CONTENTS

INTRODUCTION

❞ Teachers should use formative assessment as part of their everyday practice to help pupils achieve learning outcomes. ❞

Harlen et al (2012)

❞ Explore, Engage, Extend allows you to tailor science lessons to the children based on their questions and misconceptions. It highlights any areas where children are very confident or don't understand. ❞

Project Teacher

It is well established that effective learning is underpinned by formative assessment and that good teaching makes use of information gathered through assessment data (Black and Harrison, 2006). Earle (2014) states that 'the information gained [through assessment] should lead to an impact on learning by adaption of learning experiences.' In other words, planning should be tailored to the children's needs. Explore, Engage, Extend supports teachers to do exactly this. Each one hour carousel of highly engaging practical activities will generate rich assessment data, enabling the teacher to plan the topic in response to the children's specific needs.

Ideally a teacher will plan a topic from a starting point of knowing what it is that the children already know, what they don't know and what they would like to know. Of course, children don't necessarily know what it is that they don't know and that is where a curriculum comes in. Teachers have the complex job of working with children's existing ideas and interests while supporting them to develop their understanding of the scientific concepts set out in a curriculum.

In many science curricula, children encounter a particular science topic once every two years at most. Some topics may only be covered once in each key stage of primary school. Consequently at the start of any new topic, the children's previous formal learning is likely not to have been very recent, and they may struggle to recall key concepts and vocabulary. Added to this, where a previous teacher may have passed on information about the children's conceptual understanding at the end of a topic, these data can only be said to be valid at the time the assessment was made.

In following schemes of work or using the previous year's planning, the teacher runs the risk that the children will not make the intended progress. If the children come to their science lessons with too little prior knowledge, they can feel lost; if they already know what is being taught, they can feel bored. This is not to say that previous planning or schemes of work should be seen as redundant; far from it — they can form a useful basis for creating a set of learning experiences that meet the needs of the particular learners.

How do teachers find out what prior knowledge and understanding, and 'misconceptions' the children have? Practical science activities provide a wealth of opportunity for teachers to gather assessment data, yet many teachers use test papers or written exercises to assess children's knowledge and understanding. In addition, teacher assessment of conceptual understanding in primary science is more likely to be used at the end of a topic to establish and record what has been learned (i.e. for summative purposes), rather than as a tool to inform planning and support learning at the start (Harlen et al, 2012).

Eliciting the children's prior knowledge through specially designed practical activities enables a teacher to make more accurate and objective judgements about their prior knowledge. McMahon (2017) reminds teachers of the need to guard against the assumption that their informal knowledge of the children is sufficient, and encourages the collection of evidence to support this. Using Explore, Engage, Extend before the start of a topic will equip the teacher with a comprehensive and explicit understanding of how to ensure that the children make progress throughout the topic.

WHAT IS EXPLORE, ENGAGE, EXTEND?

Explore, Engage, Extend is a set of practical activities to support teachers with assessment for learning in science across the upper primary age range (age 7 – 11). The topics have been written based around key concepts so that they are applicable to any of the national curricula used across the UK. There are twenty topics included, which are presented as five for each year group; however, these are transferable and can be used effectively in other year groups as appropriate for the curriculum being followed by the school.

The activities have been designed to be used as pre-planning lessons. They generate rich assessment data, enabling the teacher to plan the topic in response to the children's specific needs. However, the resource could also be used at other times during a topic. The principle behind the comprehensive set of ideas is to support learning through practical activity, and to offer multiple opportunities for assessment for learning.

WHAT IS THE RATIONALE FOR EXPLORE, ENGAGE, EXTEND?

Using Explore, Engage, Extend as a framework for planning the children's next learning experiences enables a teacher to:

- Generate excitement and stimulate discussion about the topic
- Plan lessons relevant to the children's interests
- Identify misconceptions and plan learning experiences to address these
- Find out what they children would like to know
- Make explicit links between what the children already know and what is new
- Highlight relevant vocabulary

It gives the children opportunities to:

- Practise memory recall and knowledge retrieval
- Increase their engagement with the learning
- Ask more focused questions
- Take ownership of their own learning
- Recognise the value of their informal learning to their formal learning experiences

WHAT TEACHERS SAY ABOUT USING EXPLORE, ENGAGE, EXTEND

Teachers in the pilot project reported that:

- They now do more practical work in their science lessons
- They are able to target their questioning more effectively
- They were better able to plan for ALL children
- They generally think more about the needs of their children
- Their children were more motivated when they were part of the planning process
- Their children took more ownership of enquiry in science
- The activities were engaging and very easily managed

REFERENCES

Black, P. and Harrison, C. (2006) *Science inside the black box*. London: King's College.

Earle, S. (2014) 'Formative and summative assessment of science in English primary schools: evidence from the Primary Science Quality Mark.' *Research in Science & Technological Education*, 32 (2): 216-228.

Harlen, W. et al. (2012) *Developing policy, principles and practice in primary school science assessment*. London: Nuffield Foundation.

McMahon, K. (2017) Assessment of working scientifically – the TAPS Focused Assessment approach. *Primary Science Special Issue March 2018*, 15-16 ASE

RECOMMENDED READING

Earle, S. (2017) 'The challenge of balancing key principles in teacher assessment', *Journal of Emergent Science* (12) ASE

Teacher Assessment in Primary Science (TAPS) *Developing guidance and resources to support teachers and schools*. https://pstt.org.uk/resources/curriculum-materials/assessment

❝ Explore, Engage, Extend sessions provide priceless information about the children's prior knowledge which supports them and you throughout the topic ❞

Project Teacher

HOW DO I USE EXPLORE, ENGAGE, EXTEND?

TIMING

Each topic includes a set of six activities that should take around one hour in total to do. Ideally they are carried out in advance of the new topic starting, so giving the teacher time to use the data gathered to plan the lessons for the new topic.

ORGANISING THE CLASSROOM

The activities are designed to be done as a carousel, with one activity per table. Allow plenty of space around each station. Each of the six activities includes a question card and this should be placed on the table with the appropriate resources listed. All question cards can be downloaded from pstt.org.uk/eee-resources. They should be printed at A4 size so that all the children will be more likely to see them easily. Where the listed resources include pictures, these can also be downloaded from pstt.org.uk/eee-resources. Some resource cards include multiple pictures or statements that will need to be cut up and shuffled before using.

THE QUESTION CARDS

Each card has three questions:

1. Questions in pink. These are generally based on observing and describing and are designed to be accessible for all children.

2. Questions in orange. These ask children to sort or compare, or to offer further information. Sometimes they encourage more detailed observation, or ask the children to make suggestions about causes or reasons for observed phenomena.

3. Questions in green. These are more challenging and generally ask children to explain observed phenomena or relate them to real life.

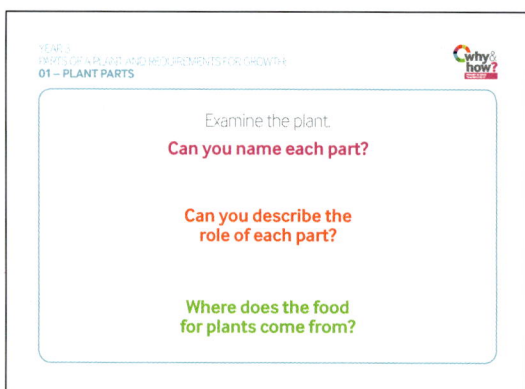

WHAT TO DO

Divide the children into six groups – ideally mixed ability .

Run briefly through each activity in order to familiarise children with each task and where necessary demonstrate how something works or how to use a particular piece of equipment. Keep this to a minimum so the children discover and work things out for themselves as much as possible.

Time the activities so that the children spend between five and ten minutes on each one, before moving to the next. (N.B. The children may need longer when this way of working is new to them.)

Listen to children's discussions or sit and observe an activity of particular interest, noting the ideas being expressed and the vocabulary used. As far as possible allow the children to carry out the activities independently.

Once the children have all explored each of the six activities, give each child a post-it note and ask them to write everything they know about the topic on it, and put their initials at the bottom. All children can then stick their post-it notes on a large piece of paper (or equivalent) labelled 'What I know'.

Then give the children a second post-it note (a different colour from the first) and ask them to write what they would like to know and put their initials at the bottom. All children can then stick their post-it notes on a large piece of paper (or equivalent) labelled 'What I would like to know'.

AFTER THE LESSON

After the lesson, look through the 'What I know' post-it notes. These will give you rich feedback about the children's current understanding. Take particular note of:

- Concepts that appear to be commonly understood
- The vocabulary used or not used
- Any misconceptions that are revealed
- Noticeable gaps that will need considering

Then look through the 'What I would like to know' post-it notes. Take particular note of:

- Questions that are commonly asked and can be grouped together
- Questions that are directly linked to planned key concepts being taught in the topic
- Other questions that might be interesting to explore

PLANNING FOR CHALLENGING CHILDREN'S MISCONCEPTIONS

Any misconceptions will need to be addressed directly by planning demonstrations or activities that will prove the misconception inaccurate, or provide evidence for the children that challenges their existing idea.

At the end of each topic in this handbook, three typical misconceptions are listed in the section 'Challenging misconceptions'. They are written on blue post-it notes and underneath each a suggestion is given about ways in which these might be addressed.

PLANNING FOR ANSWERING THE CHILDREN'S QUESTIONS

As each carousel of activities has been designed around the key concepts for each individual topic, many of the children's questions are very likely to be directly related to the content that needs to be taught. Therefore exploring answers to these questions can be reasonably easy to cover using existing planning.

For all other questions, there are several options:

1) Compile a list of the questions and share with the class. Discuss which approach would be needed for each question – research, fair test, pattern seeking, observations over time or classifying. Decide as a class which questions to investigate.

2) Give children who have already achieved the expected level in key areas the additional questions as extension tasks.

3) Set questions as homework tasks, to be investigated and answered at home. The children should be encouraged to bring in results to share with the class.

4) Bring in an expert. Some questions might be best answered by an expert. Links to scientists, engineers and academics can be made via universities or social media. Questions can be asked via Skype, social media or by letter.

At the end of each topic in this handbook, examples of three possible questions are listed in the section 'Questions children may ask'. They are written on green post-it notes and underneath each a suggestion is given about ways in which children might try and find the answers to them.

Note that the examples given of misconceptions and of questions that the children may ask are not exhaustive lists, and nor are they necessarily the most common misconceptions or questions that the children might have. They have been taken from children's post-it notes during trials of the assessment activities. They are included here to support the teacher with the process of planning for addressing misconceptions and enabling children to find answers to their own questions. Reading through the examples given will help teachers develop the confidence and skills to do this with their children's own responses.

DOWNLOAD YOUR
CLASS RESOURCES HERE:

Download a pdf of these activity cards from our website: **pstt.org.uk/eee-resources**

YEAR THREE RESOURCES

YEAR FOUR RESOURCES

YEAR FIVE RESOURCES

YEAR SIX RESOURCES

PARTS OF A PLANT AND REQUIREMENTS FOR GROWTH

Key concepts

- Flowering plants generally have the following parts: roots, stem/trunk, leaves and flowers.

- Each part performs a specific role for the plant.

- Plants need air, light, water, nutrients from soil, and room for life and growth — the precise amounts vary from plant to plant.

Key vocabulary:

Part	Seed	Soil	Cold
Role	Trunk	Fertiliser	Temperature
Leaf	Branch	Damp	Grow
Leaves	Stem	Wet	Growth
Flower	Bark	Dry	Healthy
Blossom	Stalk	Dark	Transported
Petal	Water	Light	Life cycle
Fruit	Light	Hot	Pollination
Berry	Air	Warm	Seed formation
Root	Nutrients	Cool	Seed dispersal
Bulb			

Activity	Resources required	Background knowledge	What to look out for
01	A whole plant, including roots or resource sheet PARTS OF A PLANT AND REQUIREMENTS FOR GROWTH 1	The different parts of a plant have different functions. The roots of a plant take up water and nutrients from the soil. The roots also keep the plant anchored in the soil. The stem carries water and nutrients to different parts of the plant and ensures the flower is prominent. The leaves use energy from the light from the Sun to convert carbon dioxide from the air and water from the soil into sugar, which the plant then uses as food. Some plants have flowers and these are involved in reproduction, producing seeds from which new plants grow.	Children may not know how a plant gets its food and may think it comes from the soil. Do children understand the role of each part of the plant?
02	Two+ different healthy plants.	Healthy plants have a full, bushy growth of firm, green leaves. (Leaves may be different colours depending upon the plant.) To maintain health, a plant needs air, light, water, the correct temperature and nutrients.	Do children know the requirements of healthy plant growth? Children may suggest, plants need fertiliser as this is commonly associated with healthy plants.
03	Two+ different unhealthy plants. (Place a plant in the dark for a few days and leave one without water)	Unhealthy plants may have long spindly stems with sparse leaves (lack of light). Leaves may be discoloured or wilted (lack of nutrients or light) or may dry and fall off (lack of water). To recover health, the plants need air, light, water, the correct temperature and nutrients.	Can children make sensible suggestions to help the plants to recover?
04	Resource sheet PARTS OF A PLANT AND REQUIREMENTS FOR GROWTH 4	Plants need air, light, water, nutrients and the correct temperature to be healthy. If they are healthy, they can continue making their own food out of carbon dioxide and water, using energy from the light from the Sun. Nutrients are found in soil. Some soils are more nutrient rich than others. Fertilisers contain nutrients.	Children may mistakenly believe all plants always need soil, pots, fertiliser and other items as these are commonly associated with healthy plants.
05	A range of different seeds – include peas or beans and spices. *Beware of nut allergies.	The seed of a plant contains a food store and a tiny embryo enclosed in a seed coat that protects the plant from being damaged. With the correct combination of water and temperature, the seed will begin to grow – this is called germination and the energy for this to happen comes from the seed itself. The first thing to emerge from a germinating seed is a young root. This is followed by the stem and leaves.	Do children know what is inside a seed? Do they use the word GERMINATE? Some may mistakenly believe seeds need soil and light to germinate.
06	Resource sheet PARTS OF A PLANT AND REQUIREMENTS FOR GROWTH 6	The life cycle of a flowering plant runs through the following steps in a continuous cycle: plant grows, plant flowers, flower produces fruit, fruit releases seed, seed germinates. Seeds are produced by the flower after it has been pollinated.	Can children correctly order the cycle? Do they form a cycle or do they make the sequence a terminating line that does not regenerate? Do they know where seeds come from?

LESSON ACTIVITY CARDS:

01 – PLANT PARTS

Examine the plant.

Can you name each part?

Can you describe the role of each part?

Where does the food for plants come from?

02 – HEALTHY

Examine the plants.

Describe the plants.

How are they different? How are they the same?

What do plants need to stay healthy?

03 – UNHEALTHY

Examine the plants.

Describe the plants.

How are they different? How are they the same?

What has happened to make the plant unhealthy? Could you make the plant healthy again? How?

04 – LIFE AND GROWTH

Look at the pictures.

Which of these are essential for plant life and growth?

Why?

What would happen if a plant received no light?

05 – SEEDS

Examine the seeds.

What are seeds?

How are they different, how are they the same?

What do they need to begin to grow? What is it called when seeds begin to grow?

06 – LIFE CYCLE

Look at the cards.

Can you put the cards in order?

What is happening in each part?

Where do seeds come from?

Download a pdf of these activity cards from our website:
pstt.org.uk/eee-resources

CHALLENGING MISCONCEPTIONS:

1) Roots take food from the soil for the plant.

2) Leaves take in water.

3) Sunlight keeps plants warm.

1) Leaves absorb the Sun's energy to create their own food. Water and minerals are taken in through the roots and air through the leaves.

• Grow soil-less bean and pea plants in plastic bags or jars filled with wet paper towel. Grow cress on damp paper towel. Are the plants healthy? Where are they getting food from?

2) Water is taken in through the roots.

• Observe roots using a microscope – root hairs take up water.

• Set up a bare-rooted plant in a clear jar. Cover the surface of the water with a layer of oil so the water cannot evaporate. Cover with a clear plastic bag. Can water get to the leaves? Leave overnight and observe. What happens to the water in the jar? What happens to the plastic bag? Explain that water has been taken in by the roots, moves through the plant through tiny tubes, and is then given out (transpired) by the leaves – just like we drink water, it travels around our body in blood vessels and then is either perspired through our skin or passed in our urine.

3) The leaves use light from the Sun, along with carbon dioxide from the air and water to make food for the plant.

• Cover some of the leaves of a plant with black paper and leave for three days. Uncover and compare covered leaves with uncovered leaves. How have the leaves with no Sun been affected? How are they different from the uncovered leaves?

• Research why some plants lose their leaves in the autumn.

QUESTIONS CHILDREN MAY ASK:

1) What is inside a seed?

2) Where do seeds come from?

3) Are trees plants?

1) A seed is a small plant embryo enclosed in a covering called the seed coat, usually with some stored food.

- Soak some pea and bean seeds in water overnight. Compare dried peas and beans with the soaked ones. What differences are found? Pick up a soaked bean and examine it. What will the inside of the seed look like? Why? Rub the soaked bean between fingers. The seed coat should rub off. Why is the seed coat important? Now split the seed in two. (There is a slit going down the middle of the seed where it should come apart with a little help). Observe the inside. Describe and/or draw what you see. Were your predictions correct? Leave and re-examine once dried.

- Observe seeds using a hand lens. Choose a large seed, e.g. a bean and draw and label key parts that can be observed.

- Investigate how the inside of a seed changes over time by germinating a batch of beans and dissecting one every day.

2) Plants produce flowers to make seeds. To make a seed a flower must be pollinated. Pollen from one flower travels to another flower, where the seeds are made. The petals act like an advertisement to attract various animals, which will carry the pollen from one flower to another. When a bee or other insect lands on a flower, it uses its long tube-shaped tongue (called a proboscis) like a straw to drink the sweet nectar inside the flower. This nectar is eventually turned into honey by the bees at the hive. While the bee is busy getting a drink, tiny grains of pollen often get stuck to the bee. When a bee flies to a different flower to get more nectar, some of the pollen grains will fall off the bee and onto the new flower, then the second flower will be pollinated and a fruit and seeds will develop.

- Introduce different pollinators by decorating wings to wear. The most common pollinators in the UK are bees, moths and butterflies.

- Create some large flowers with colourful petals to attract pollinators. On the reverse, draw seeds.

- Play 'Pollinator Tag'. Three children are chosen as pollinators and can wear their wings. The rest of the class are flowers and use double sided sticky tape to stick a cotton wool ball to their flower for pollen. Pollinators to chase the flowers. If a flower is caught the pollinator takes their pollen. If the pollinator is already holding pollen from another flower, they must give it to the flower they caught. The flower is now pollinated – the player sits down, they turn over the flower to produce seeds. The game ends when all flowers are pollinated and have produced seeds.

- Spot pollinators and flowers in the school grounds or local area. Identify bees, moths, butterflies. Play colour bingo – tick off flower colours as they are visited by pollinators.

3) Plants are living things that grow on land or in water. All plants make their own food, taking energy from sunlight. Unlike animals, plants cannot move from place to place and most are rooted in the ground. Trees are plants – they cannot move from one place to another and they have the ability to create their own food. Trees only differ as they have a trunk – a thick, wooden stem.

- Compare the parts of a common plant, e.g. bean or sunflower, with the parts of a tree. Which parts do they have in common? Which parts are different? What role do these parts play?

- Compare leaves from a tree and a bean/sunflower plant. What is different? What is the same? What do you think the role of a tree's leaf is?

- Grow a tree from a seed (sycamore seeds germinate easily) alongside growing a sunflower or bean – both in wet paper towel at first so germination is visible, then plant in compost. How do the processes compare? What is the same? What is different?

- Thinking question – how does a tree get its food?

01 – PLANT PARTS

YEAR 3
PARTS OF A PLANT AND REQUIREMENTS FOR GROWTH:
01 – PLANT PARTS

why & how?

Examine the plant.

Can you name each part?

Can you describe the role of each part?

Where does the food for plants come from?

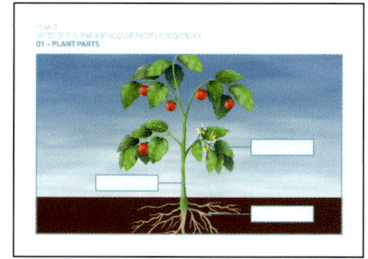

04 – LIFE AND GROWTH

YEAR 3
PARTS OF A PLANT AND REQUIREMENTS FOR GROWTH:
04 – LIFE AND GROWTH

why & how?

Look at the pictures.

Which of these are essential for plant life and growth?

Why?

What would happen if a plant received no light?

SOIL	AIR	POTS
COLD	WATER	FERTILISER
SUNLIGHT	COMPOST	SAND
WARMTH	SPACE	NUTRIENTS

06 – LIFE CYCLE

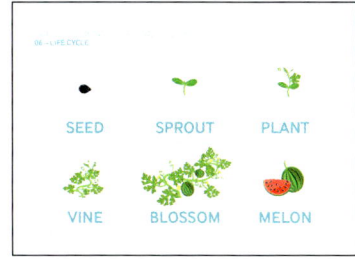

SEED   SPROUT   PLANT

VINE   BLOSSOM   MELON

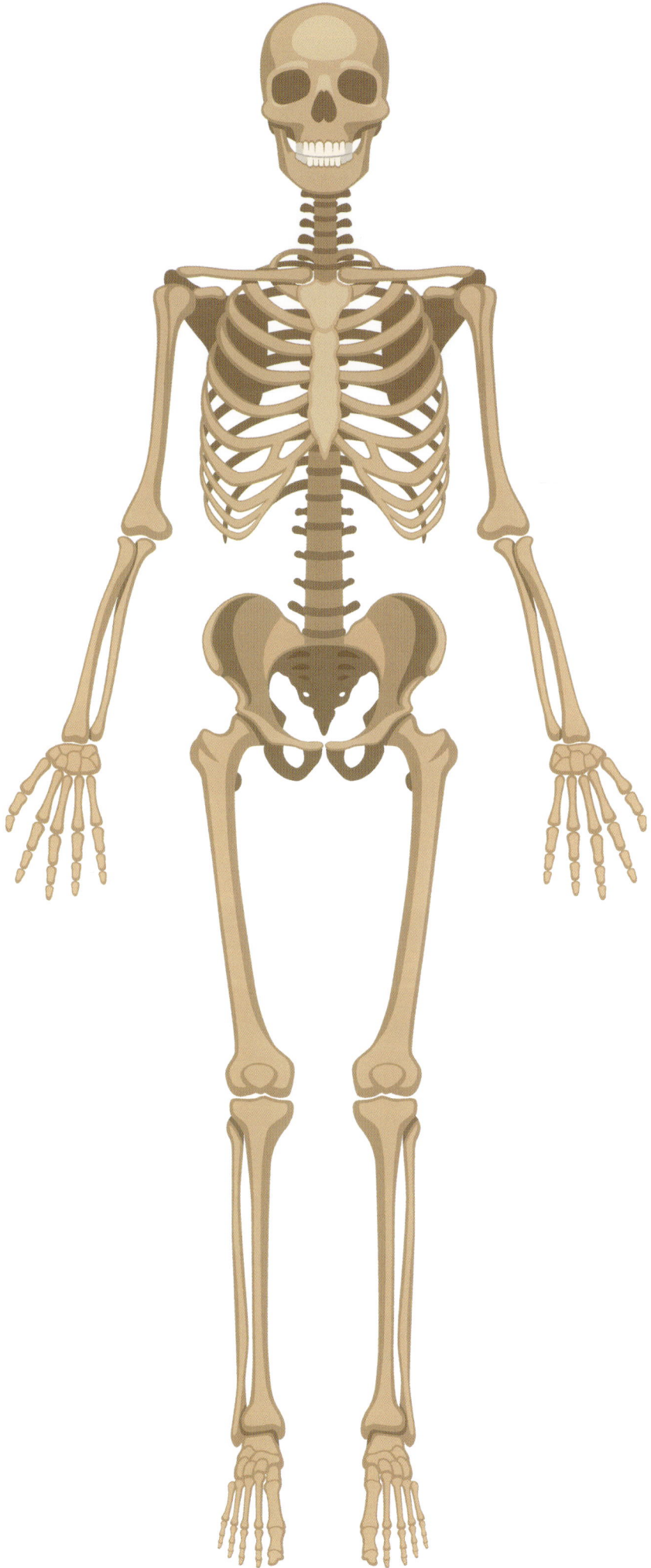

NUTRITION AND SKELETON

Key concepts

- Animals, including humans, need the right types and amount of nutrition; they cannot make their own food and they get nutrition from what they eat.

- Humans and some other animals have skeletons and muscles for support, protection and movement.

Key vocabulary:

Nutrition	Carbohydrate	Skeleton	Spine
Nutrient	Protein	Muscles	Vertebrate
Food types	Vitamin	Support	Invertebrate
Fruit and vegetables	Mineral	Protection	Joint
	Fibre	Movement	Socket
Dairy food	Water	Skull	Bone
Fat	Balanced diet	Ribs	Tendon
Sugar			

Activity	Resources required	Background knowledge	What to look out for
01	**Selection of drinks, foods and/or food packaging – try to include a range of tinned, processed, fresh, dried, healthy and unhealthy.**	Our bodies need a balanced diet to work properly. Good health involves drinking enough water and eating the right amount of items from the four main food groups. Foods high in saturated fats, salt and sugar should be eaten in moderation, whereas foods high in fibre, vitamins and minerals and starch should be eaten in greater quantities. Too much sugar, fat and salt can lead to obesity, tooth decay, diabetes, heart attack, high blood pressure or dementia.	Can children pick out the foods that are unhealthy? Do they know why they are unhealthy – do they mention sugar, fat or salt?
02	**Examples of food packaging with traffic light info on the front.**	Food may be labelled with a traffic light label showing how much fat, saturated fats, sugar and salt are in that food by using the traffic light signals for high (red), medium (amber) and low (green) content for each of these ingredients. The percentages indicate how much of an adult's recommended daily intake is provided.	Do children understand the colours, weights and/or percentages?
03	**Resource sheet NUTRITION AND SKELETON 3**	The four main food groups are carbohydrates, proteins, fats, vitamins and minerals. Carbohydrates are an energy source and are found in starchy foods, e.g bread, potatoes and pasta. Proteins help our bodies to repair themselves and are found in e.g. fish, meat, nuts, seeds, eggs and cheese. Fats, found in e.g. butter, cheese and oil, give our bodies energy that can be stored and provide a layer under our skin to keep us warm. Vitamins and minerals are needed for many things, e.g. healing wounds, building strong bones and teeth, making blood, and keeping our brain working. Vitamins and minerals are found in e.g. fruits, vegetables, fish and milk. Fibre (sometimes called roughage) is the indigestible part of our food, e.g. apple skins, bran husks found in wholemeal flour, and is essential for the health of our intestine as it helps the food move through it.	Do children understand the terms 'carbohydrate', 'protein', 'fat', 'vitamins' and 'minerals'? Do they know in which foods each can be found and why they benefit the body?
04	**Resource sheet NUTRITION AND SKELETON 4**	Many animals, including humans, have skeletons to support and protect their bodies and to help them move. The human skeleton is made of bone. Bones grow as we grow. Our skull protects our brain and our ribs protect our heart and lungs.	Children may only draw bones they can feel, such as ribs and skull. Do children realise that the bones in our bodies are connected? Can they name any? Do they know the functions of bones?
05	**Resource sheet NUTRITION AND SKELETON 5**	Animals can be classified as either vertebrates or invertebrates. Vertebrates are animals that have a backbone/spine inside their bodies. Vertebrates include fish, amphibians, reptiles, birds and mammals. Invertebrates are animals that don't have a backbone. Some have soft bodies, like worms and jellyfish. Other invertebrates, such as insects and crustaceans, have a hard outer casing called an exoskeleton. This protects their bodies a bit like a suit of armour.	Children may think that animals without legs such as snakes do not have a backbone and be unaware that insects, and other invertebrates with legs, do not.
06	**Resource sheet NUTRITION AND SKELETON 6**	In vertebrates, muscles are attached to bones. When a muscle contracts (bunches up), it gets shorter and so pulls up the bone it is attached to. When a muscle relaxes, it goes back to its normal size. This causes movement. In animals with exoskeletons, muscles are attached to key parts of the exoskeleton, these then relax and contract for movement. Other invertebrates use a range of strategies, including jet propulsion (jellyfish and squid).	Children may be unaware that bones are moved by muscles – they may not realise they are connected. Do they realise that there are different mechanisms for movement?

LESSON ACTIVITY CARDS:

01 – FOOD SORT

Examine the foods.

**Sort the foods into 'healthy',
'unhealthy' and 'not sure'.**

Why are some foods unhealthy?

What do these foods do to our bodies?

---

02 – PACKAGING

Examine the front of the packaging.

What does the packaging tell you about the food?

What tells you how healthy it is?

What do the percentages mean?

---

03 – FOOD GROUPS

Examine the cards.

**Which of these foods should we eat a lot of?
Which of these foods should we only have
in small amounts?**

**Which food group best describes
the food in the picture?**

**Why is each of these food groups
important for our body?**

---

04 – BONES

Draw and label the bones in your body.

What are bones made of?

Why do we need bones?

---

05 – SKELETONS

Examine the cards.

**Sort the animals into two groups – those with
a skeleton inside their bodies and those without**

What do the others have instead?

Do you know the name for each group?

---

06 – MOVEMENT

Look at the cards.

How does each animal move?

What parts of the body help it to move?

Which one is the odd one out and why?

Download a pdf of these activity cards from our website:
pstt.org.uk/eee-resources

CHALLENGING MISCONCEPTIONS:

1) Snakes don't have a skeleton.

2) Cheese is bad for you.

3) Diet drinks are good for you.

1) Snakes do have bones. Animals with bones are known as vertebrates – snakes are vertebrates. A snake's backbone is made up of between 200-400 vertebrae attached to ribs. That is what makes them so flexible and helps them move along!.

• Find pictures of different animal skeletons, including a snake, and ask children to match them to the correct animal. How did they decide which animal matched which skeleton? What did they use to help?

• Compare snake vertebrae to a human's. How are they the same? How are they different?

2) Cheese is a dairy product derived from milk. It contains nutrients such as calcium, protein, phosphorus, zinc, vitamin A and vitamin B12. The high-quality protein in cheese provides the body with essential building blocks for strong muscles. However, cheese is also loaded with fat, sodium and cholesterol. Typical cheeses are 70 percent fats, mainly saturated ("bad") fats. All of these nutrients are essential for good health and only become a problem when you eat too much.

• Create a PMI (plus, minus and interesting) fact sheet for each important nutrient. Plus – how do they help our body? Minus –how can they harm our body if we have too little or too much? Interesting – an interesting fact about the nutrient or source of nutrient. Even water can be bad for you if you drink too much!

• Investigate the EATWELL plate and the recommended proportions of each food groups. Design a healthy meal using this as a template.

• Explore food packaging – look at the traffic light and nutritional information on the front and the back. Using packaging, each child should create a Top Trump card for a food item with sugar, saturated fat, protein, salt, starch, fibre amounts listed. Play a game as a class. Sit in a circle with each child's food item clearly visible to the rest of the class – this could be the actual food item or its picture/name written on a piece of card. One child begins by choosing a nutrient then challenging a class mate. For protein, starch, fibre, the highest amount wins. For salt, sugar and saturated fat, the lowest amount wins. Winner stays in charge of the game.

3) Diet drinks contain no sugar, unlike regular drinks. They contain a sweetener (often aspartame) instead. However, this does not mean that they are good for your health. There is no nutritional value in most carbonated drinks – no protein, no starch, no fibre, no vitamins or minerals. Also, the carbon dioxide used to make these drinks fizzy also makes them slightly acidic and can cause damage your teeth.

• Compare the nutritional value of a range of common drinks – milk, water, fresh fruit juice, cola, diet cola, squash. If possible, using pH sticks, test the pH of each. Order from least beneficial to most. Reorder from most acidic to least. Compare the order of both sets. Which drink would you recommend children drink and why? Finally, reorder according to preference – from least preferred to most. What makes a drink popular? How could we use this to make healthy drinks more popular?

QUESTIONS CHILDREN MAY ASK:

1) What are bones made of?

2) Why does food make us fat?

3) How do worms move?

1) Bones are made of mineral salts, calcium, proteins and water. Bone is living, growing tissue. Collagen is an elastic protein that provides a framework, and calcium phosphate is a mineral that adds strength and hardens the framework. This combination of collagen and calcium makes bone strong and flexible enough to withstand stress. If we don't eat enough calcium, our bones become weak.

• You will need:
– A piece of red wool about 30 cm long
– A piece of blue wool about 30 cm long
– Some play dough – red or pink is best
– A piece of bread with the crusts cut off
– A piece of white or cream cardboard
– Straws
– PVA glue
– Sticky tape
– Scissors

The play dough is our bone marrow. Bone marrow is a soft tissue that sits in the centre of our bone. There are two types of bone marrow: red bone marrow – this makes blood cells and yellow bone marrow – this contains fat cells. When we are born almost all our bone marrow is red; as we get older that changes and, as adults, only around half our bone marrow contains red bone marrow. The blue wool represents a vein. The red wool represents an artery. Blood flows through your arteries to bring nutrients and oxygen and veins take waste away. This is to keep bones healthy and alive!

Flatten out your play dough a bit and place the blue wool and the red wool on top, then roll your play dough around the wool.

Now we need our spongy bone. This is the part of your bone that is mostly made up of collagen; it has a structure full of holes to keep the bone strong but light and flexible. If our bones were completely solid, it would be difficult to move as they would be so heavy! The slice of bread represents the spongy bone, wrapped around the 'bone marrow'.

Around the spongy bone is a layer called the compact bone. This layer is full of hollow rods made of calcium mostly acting as reinforcement to protect the bone marrow. To represent the compact bone layer, use a piece of thin cardboard, 15cm by 15cm. Spread PVA glue all over one side of the cardboard and stick down straws, all cut to 15cm in length. Use sticky tape to ensure it remains stuck down.

Roll the compact bone around the spongy bone layer for a finished model.

2) The main cause of putting on weight is an imbalance between calories consumed and calories expended – eating too much and exercising too little.

• Investigate food packaging and look at the calories provided by different foods.

• Research the recommended calorie intake for children.

• Ask children to list their favourite take-away meal and work out the calorie content using their online nutrition calculator.

• Use the British Heart Foundation's exercise calorie calculator to work out how much exercise is needed to use up calories consumed in the children's favourite meal. Compare different exercises, e.g. which burns the most calories...dancing, cycling or jogging?

3) Earthworms have bristles in groups around or under their body. They travel through underground tunnels or move on the soil surface by using their bristles as anchors, and pushing themselves forward or backward using strong stretching and contracting muscles.

• Using a tray lined with wet paper towel, observe earthworms using hand lenses. Compare with pictures in reference books. Can children spot the saddle (clitellum), bristles (setae) and segments? Which end is the mouth? Observe how the worm moves. Focus on one segment – how does it change shape?

• Make a model earthworm using a water-filled long balloon. Squeeze the back end of the balloon and hold (this represents the muscle of a segment contracting). What happens to the front? Hold down the front of the balloon (this represents the bristles anchoring the front in the ground) and release the back end (muscles relax). What happens to the back end of the balloon? To make movement more obvious, this can be done on squared paper, marking the starting positions of both ends.

03 – FOOD GROUPS

YEAR 3
NUTRITION AND SKELETON:
03 – FOOD GROUPS

why&
how?

Examine the cards.

Which of these foods should we eat a lot of?
**Which of these foods should we only have
in small amounts?**

**Which food group best describes
the food in the picture?**

**Why is each of these food groups
important for our body?**

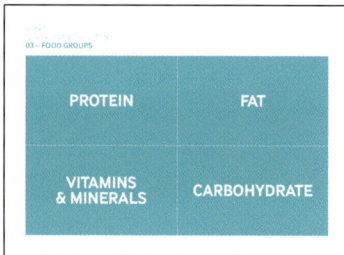

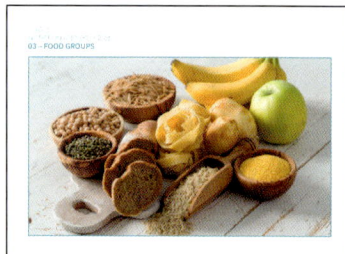

04 – BONES

why&
how?

Draw and label the bones in your body.

What are bones made of?

Why do we need bones?

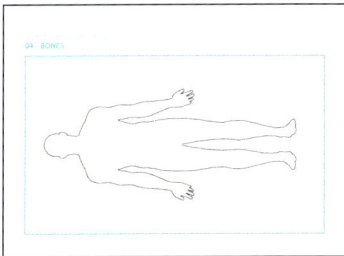

04 – BONES

05 – SKELETONS

why & how?

Examine the cards.

Sort the animals into two groups – those with a skeleton inside their bodies and those without

What do the others have instead?

Do you know the name for each group?

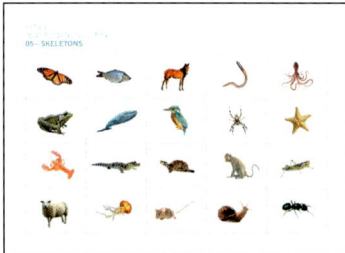

06 – MOVEMENT

YEAR 3
NUTRITION AND SKELETON
06 – MOVEMENT

why &
how?

Look at the cards.

How does each animal move?

What parts of the body help it to move?

Which one is the odd one out and why?

ROCKS AND SOILS

Key concepts

- Rocks can be grouped together on the basis of their appearance and simple physical properties.

- Fossils are formed when things that have lived are trapped within rock.

- Soils are made from rocks and organic matter.

Key vocabulary:

Rock	Fossil	Marble
Sedimentary	Grain	Chalk
Igneous	Crystal	Granite
Metamorphic	Hard	Sandstone
Smooth	Soft	Slate
Rough	Texture	Sand
Light	Permeable	Clay
Soil	Impermeable	Peat

Activity	Resources required	Background knowledge	What to look out for
01	Two or three samples of the same rock, hand lenses.	Rocks are naturally occurring objects containing more than one mineral. Different rocks have different physical properties depending on their composition and how they were formed.	Are children using words such as 'hard/soft', 'grains', 'crystals', 'light/heavy', 'layers', 'sandy', 'opaque', 'translucent', 'smooth/rough'?
02	A selection of different rocks, hand lenses.	Rocks can be classified by comparing their appearance: • layers (foliation) • colour • grain size and their properties: • reflection of light (lustre) • hardness • permeable/impermeable.	As above.
03	Resource sheet ROCKS AND SOILS 3 or real examples of each item shown.	A fossil is the preserved remains or traces of a dead plant or animal. The process by which a fossil is formed is called 'fossilisation'. Things like footprints, eggs and even poo can be fossilised too (it is then called coprolite). Manmade items cannot be fossilised.	Children can confuse historical artefacts and fossils. They can also be unaware that fossils of plants, insects, birds and other living things have been found – not just fossils of dinosaurs.
04	Resource sheet ROCKS AND SOILS 4	After an animal or plant dies, the soft parts decompose leaving the hard parts behind, e.g. an animal's skeleton. This becomes buried by small particles of rock called sediment. As layers of sediment build up on top, the sediment around the skeleton begins to compact and turn to rock. The hard parts are gradually dissolved by water seeping through the rock. Minerals in the water replace the hard parts, leaving a rock replica of the original, called a fossil.	Can children sequence the cards correctly? Can they describe the process?
05	Soil sample, not dried. Hand lenses. *Wash hands thoroughly after this activity.	Soil is a mixture of tiny particles of rock, dead plants and animals (humus), air and water. Different soils have different properties depending on their composition. Sandy soil is pale, that little humus and large particles which create lots of small air gaps. Water drains through them easily.	Do children know that soil is made of different materials? What words are they using to describe the soil?
06	Two different soil samples, not dried. Hand lenses. (Check garden centres if samples cannot be sourced locally.) *Wash hands thoroughly after this activity.	Clay soil is full of humus, with small particles. It contains very few air gaps, so water does not drain through it easily. Chalky soil is light brown and often stony and free draining. Peat does not contain any rock particles. It's made from very old decayed plants and is dark, crumbly and rich in nutrients.	

LESSON ACTIVITY CARDS:

01 – OBSERVING ROCKS

Observe the rock carefully.

Which words could you use to describe how it looks?

Which words could you use to describe how it feels?

What could this rock be used for? Why?

02 – SORTING ROCKS

Observe the rock carefully.

Sort the rocks into groups.

What heading would you give each group?

Can you sort them a different way? How many different ways can you sort them?

03 – IDENTIFYING FOSSILS

Look at the cards.

Which of these have been found as fossils?

Where are fossils found?

How are fossils formed?

04 – SEQUENCING FOSSILISATION

Look carefully at the cards.

Can you put them into the correct order?

Can you describe what is happening in each?

How long does it take for fossils to form?

05 – OBSERVING SOIL

Observe the soil carefully.

What words would you use to describe this soil?

What is soil made from?

Is all soil the same? Why/why not?

06 – COMPARING SOILS

Observe these soils carefully.

What is the same about them?

What is different?

Why are these soils different?

Download a pdf of these activity cards from our website:
pstt.org.uk/eee-resources

CHALLENGING MISCONCEPTIONS:

1) All rocks are hard.

2) Roman coins are fossils.

3) Soil is compost.

1) The word 'hard' is used differently in everyday language and children can be shown that there are degrees of hardness using the Mohs hardness scale. Rocks such as chalk and soapstone are considered soft rocks.

• If a rock can be scratched by a fingernail, it has a hardness of <2.5 Mohs. If a rock cannot be scratched by a fingernail but can be scratched by a copper penny (1982 or earlier), it has a hardness of >2.5 Mohs but < 3 Mohs. If a rock cannot be scratched by a fingernail or a copper penny but can be scratched by a steel nail, it has a hardness of between 3 and 5.5 Mohs. If a rock cannot be scratched by a steel nail, it is harder than 5.5 Mohs.

2) Fossils are traces of living things... animals, plants, footprints, poo and eggs. Historical manmade objects excavated from the ground are called artefacts.

• Hold a spoof quiz – 'artefact or fossil ' – to embed this difference and reinforce the language, showing a range of pictures such as those in the assessment task. Children to hold up Historical Artefact OR Fossil depending on picture shown. Discuss answers.

3) Soil is a mixture of rock particles, humus, water and air. Compost is a mix of humus, water and air.

• Soil surveys are great for illustrating differences in soils, which may seem quite similar to children. Tests include observations on colour and texture plus tests on drainability, pH, water content and presence of calcium carbonate.

• Use a digital microscope to observe particles in the soil.

• Dissolve soils in water and observe the different sediments formed.

QUESTIONS CHILDREN MAY ASK:

1) How are rocks made?

2) How long do fossils take to form?

3) How is soil different to compost?

1) There are three main rock types – sedimentary, igneous and metamorphic. Each of these are formed in different ways as part of the rock cycle.

• Represent the rock cycle using Starburst sweet.

Sedimentary rocks are formed when particles of rock that have been eroded from larger rocks are carried in streams and rivers to lakes and seas and sink to the bottom as sediment. As more and more layers of sediment piles on top, the weight of the sediment and water compresses the particles to form sedimentary rocks. Weather or erode particles of rock by snipping small pieces from the Starburst. Once the sweets have been weathered/eroded and piled up, press the particles with your hand against a table to form sedimentary rock.

Metamorphic rocks are formed when the movement of the Earth's crust drags rocks beneath and they are exposed to extreme heat and pressure. Create extreme pressure and heat by squeezing your sedimentary rock between both hands until it warms and the particles fuse together.

Igneous rocks are formed in volcanoes. The rock melts due to extreme heat to form magma. Igneous rocks can cool underground, or be formed when lava cools after a volcanic eruption. Use a microwave oven to melt the metamorphic rock and then leave to cool. (Adults only)

The Starburst rocks share many similar features with the rocks they represent.

2) There is no precise time frame for fossilisation and it depends on the size of the remains and the prevailing conditions. Fossils are defined as the remains or traces of organisms that died more than 10,000 years ago. Therefore, by definition the minimum time it takes to make a fossil is 10,000 years.

3) See strategies for misconception 3 on page 35.

03 — IDENTIFYING FOSSILS

why&
how?

Look at the cards.

Which of these have been found as fossils?

Where are fossils found?

How are fossils formed?

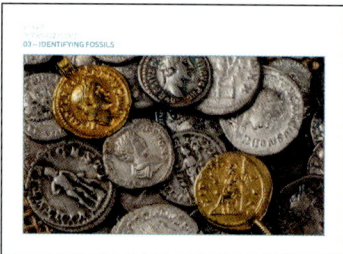

03 — IDENTIFYING FOSSILS

03 — IDENTIFYING FOSSILS

03 — IDENTIFYING FOSSILS

03 — IDENTIFYING FOSSILS

03 — IDENTIFYING FOSSILS

03 — IDENTIFYING FOSSILS

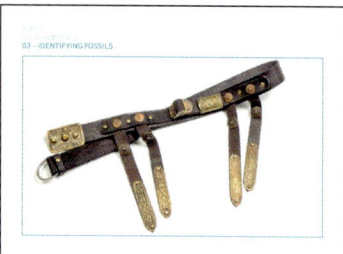

03 — IDENTIFYING FOSSILS

04 – SEQUENCING FOSSILISATION

LIGHT AND MATERIALS

Key concepts

- Dark is the absence of light.

- Light is needed in order to see things.

- Light is reflected by materials.

- Light travels through some materials and not others.

- Shadows are formed when the light from a light source is blocked by an opaque object.

- The size of shadows change according to the size of the object and the relative positions of the object and the light source.

- Light from the Sun can be dangerous and there are ways to protect their eyes.

Key vocabulary:

Light	Mirror	Sun
Light source	Shadow	Torch
Dark	Block	Lamp
Darkness	Direction	Flame
Reflect	Opaque	Light bulb
Reflective	Transparent	
Rays	Translucent	

Activity	Resources required	Background knowledge	What to look out for
01	**Resource sheet LIGHT AND MATERIALS 1**	Light sources emit light. Some objects such as the Moon, mirrors, water, do not emit light but look luminous because they reflect light well. The Moon reflects the light of the Sun.	Children confuse light sources and reflectors. Can children sort light sources from reflectors of light?
02	**Resource sheet LIGHT AND MATERIALS 2**	We see things because light travels from light sources to our eyes or from light sources to objects and then to our eyes. If there is no light, we cannot see anything. Complete absence of light is very seldom experienced by children and when they use the word 'dark' they are usually describing 'very little light'.	Children can think of sight as an active process of our eyes. Do children recognise that we need light in order to see, not just our eyes? Can they use the term 'dark' correctly?
03	**Six to ten different materials – some very reflective, some not reflective and some in between.**	When light hits materials the light is either absorbed, reflected or transmitted. Most materials reflect some light or we wouldn't be able to see them. Transparent materials transmit most of the light – it is re-emitted on the opposite side. Pale and bright colours reflect light better, whereas dark colours tend to absorb more rays. Very smooth surfaces reflect light in a more regular way and appear shiny.	Are children using the words 'reflect/reflective'? Do children understand the light is 'bouncing off' the reflective materials?
04	**Resource sheet LIGHT AND MATERIALS 4**	Light from the Sun is dangerous. Too much ultra-violet light burns our skin and can ultimately cause skin cancer. It can also damage our eyes causing eye pain, cataracts, short sightedness, far sightedness and temporary loss of vision. Looking directly at the Sun damages your retina and can lead to blindness.	Do children understand the risks the Sun presents to their skin and eyes? Can children explain how to protect their skin and eyes?
05	**Set up a lamp so it is shining on a vertical surface covered with a piece of paper. Place an opaque object between the light and the paper so that a shadow is cast onto the paper.**	A shadow is made when an object blocks light; since light can't get to the area behind the object blocking it, a shadow appears. The shadow appears on the side of the object furthest from the light source. The object must be opaque or translucent to make a shadow. A transparent object will not make any shadow, as light will pass straight through it.	Do children recognise that objects block light to cause shadows? Can they name/locate an object that would not cause a shadow?
06	**Set up a lamp in the same way as activity 05, using an object that can be moved closer to and further from the light source.**	The size of the shadow depends on the angle at which the light is falling on the object and the distance between the light source and object. If the light source is directly above the object, there is little or no shadow. If the light source is perpendicular to the object the shadow is longer/larger. If an object is moved closer to the light source, the shadow gets bigger. If an object is moved further away from the light source, the shadow gets smaller.	Can children suggest ways in which to change the size and shape of the shadow? Do children think that shadows can be different colours?

LESSON ACTIVITY CARDS:

01 – IDENTIFYING LIGHT SOURCES

Look at the pictures.

**Which of these items give out light?
Which do not?**

Can you name another light source?

What is the difference between
sunlight and moonlight?

02 – HOW WE SEE

Look at the picture.

What things in the picture help us to see?

Where does the light come from?

What could we see if there was no light?

03 – COMPARING REFLECTIVE MATERIALS

Explore the materials by shining a torch on them.

**Can you sort the items into order
from least shiny to most shiny?**

What happens to light when
it hits shiny objects?

What do all shiny objects have in common?

04 – PROTECTING OURSELVES FROM THE SUN

How can the Sun harm us?

How can we protect ourselves
from the Sun's rays?

Can you think of more than one answer
to the questions above?

05 – CREATING SHADOWS

Draw round the shadow created by the object.
Describe the shadow.

What causes the shadow?

Do all objects create shadows?
Which do? Which do not?

06 – CHANGING SHADOWS

Describe the shadow.

How could you change the
size of the shadow?

Could you change the colour
or shape of the shadow? How?

Download a pdf of these activity cards from our website:
pstt.org.uk/eee-resources

CHALLENGING MISCONCEPTIONS:

1) I see things because my eyes look at them.

2) The Moon is a source of light.

3) We can see in the dark but not as well.

1+3) Children can think of sight as an active process of our eyes and do not understand that light needs to be emitted or reflected from an object into our eyes in order for us to see things. Children do not use the term 'dark' correctly. Dark means complete absence of light.

- Ask children to press a cardboard tube against some text and put one eye gently against the other end. What can they see? Can they read the text? Next, ask children to cut a small notch in the end of the tube against the text. What can they see? Can they read the text?

  We see things because light travels from light sources to our eyes or from light sources to objects and then is reflected to our eyes – no light means no sight.

- Model the reflection of light – to see a table, light hits the table and is reflected into our eyes. Use a ball to show the path of light – bounce it off the table and into a hoop representing our eye.

2) Children think reflective surfaces emit light. The Moon does not emit light but reflects light from the Sun. The Moon consists of an iron core and rocky crust, unlike the Sun, which consists of burning gases.

- Check a range of materials to see if they emit light by placing a cardboard tube against them one at a time and put one eye gently against the other end. Can you see light?

- Sort materials into shiny and not shiny. Compare shiny materials. What is the same about them? (Surface)

- Test how much light is reflected by a range of materials using a reflectivity tester (see diagram).

- Compare light reflected by smooth aluminium foil and crumpled aluminium foil.

QUESTIONS CHILDREN MAY ASK:

1) How does the Sun produce light?

2) How are shadows made?

3) Why do shadows change?

1) Hydrogen gas reacting at the core of the Sun creates energy in the form of heat and light. The light reaches us in just eight minutes. Light can be also produced by chemical reactions.

- Children can investigate glow sticks – a chemical reaction inside the glow stick creates energy given off as light. Explore how this occurs in glow sticks. Design a fair test to see how temperature affects the brightness of the glow stick.

2) Shadows are formed when light is blocked by an object.

- Challenge children to find objects they think will block light (opaque), objects they think will block some light (translucent) and objects they think will allow light to pass through (transparent). Write predictions and then test. Compare shadows formed by each. Compare properties of opaque, translucent and transparent materials.

- Create puppets for a shadow puppet show, watching how the shadow moves as the puppet moves.

- Create shadow art, using random objects to create an image e.g.

3) Shadows will change size and direction as the position of the light source, the position of the object and the angle of the light change.

- Children can use torches and objects to spot patterns between distance of object from light source and size of shadow.

- Children can draw round and measure their changing shadow throughout the day as the angle of the Sun changes.

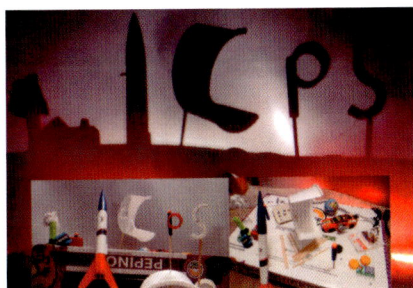

01 – IDENTIFYING LIGHT SOURCES

02 – HOW WE SEE

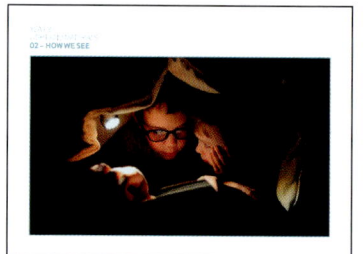

04 — PROTECTING OURSELVES FROM THE SUN

YEAR 3
LIGHT AND MATERIALS
04 — PROTECTING OURSELVES FROM THE SUN

why&
how?

How can the Sun harm us?

**How can we protect ourselves
from the Sun's rays?**

**Can you think of more than one answer
to the questions above?**

04 — PROTECTING OURSELVES FROM THE SUN

FORCES AND MAGNETS

Key concepts

- Push and pull forces can make things start and stop moving.

- Different surfaces affect how easily things move over them.

- Some forces need contact between two objects, but magnetic forces can act at a distance.

- Magnets attract some materials and not others.

- Magnets have two poles.

- Magnets attract or repel each other.

Key vocabulary:

Force	Friction	Horseshoe	Attract
Push	Magnetic	magnet	Repel
Pushing	Non-magnetic	Strength	Metal
Pull	Magnet	Poles	Iron
Pulling	Bar magnet	North pole	Steel
Contact	Ring magnet	South pole	
Non-contact	Button magnet	Material	

Activity	Resources required	Background knowledge	What to look out for
01	Resource sheet FORCES AND MAGNETS 1	Forces are pushes or pulls. Push and pull forces can make things start and stop moving, make a moving object change direction, and change the shape of objects.	Children may think that only animate objects can exert a force
02	Three wooden blocks – identical in size and shape – the bottom of one plain, the bottom of another covered in foil, and the bottom the final one covered in sandpaper. A smooth slope.	Friction is a force between two surfaces that are sliding across each other. Friction always works in the opposite direction to which the object is moving and slows the moving object down. The amount of friction depends on the surface of the objects. The rougher the surface, the more friction is produced.	Do children use the word 'friction'? Are they aware of its effects? Some children may think the smoothest surface has no friction.
03	A range of materials including several different metals.	Magnetic materials are always made of metal, but not all metals are magnetic. Iron, steel (an alloy of iron and carbon), nickel and cobalt are magnetic. Most other metals, for example aluminium, copper and gold, are NOT magnetic.	Many children will mistakenly believe that all metals are magnetic.
04	A strong magnet and magnetic object.	A magnet exerts a pull force on magnetic materials – we call this attraction. The magnet and material will stick together. Magnets are used in many different ways in our everyday life, for example, toys, credit cards, computers, compasses, some medical equipment, fridge doors, Maglev trains.	Do children use the words 'attract' and 'pull'? Can they name some everyday uses of magnets?
05	A range of different types of magnets.	There are many different kinds of magnets with a great variety of levels of strength. Strong magnets will create bigger pushing or pulling forces than weak magnets. Some magnets are barely strong enough to hold paper to a refrigerator. Others are strong enough to lift cars. The strength of a magnet is determined by the material it is made of and the strength of the external magnetic field applied.	Children may mistakenly believe the size of the magnet determines its strength and that larger magnets are stronger.
06	Two bar magnets.	When two magnets are close, they create pushing or pulling forces on one another. The two ends of a magnet are known as the north pole and the south pole. If you put two magnets together with the same poles pointing towards one another, the magnets will repel – push away from each other. If you put two magnets together with different poles pointing towards one another, the magnets will attract – pull towards each other.	Are children using the words attract, 'repel' and 'poles'?

LESSON ACTIVITY CARDS:

---

01 – PUSHES AND PULLS

Examine the cards.

**Talk about what is happening
in each card.**

**Sort the cards into pushes,
pulls, both and not sure.**

**Can you think of another
example for each category?**

---

02 – DIFFERENT SURFACES

Examine the surface of the blocks.
Place them at the top of the slope and raise it, slowly and steadily.

How are the surfaces different?

**Which block slides down first?
Which block slides down last?**

Why?

---

03 – MATERIALS

Examine the materials.

Can you name each material?

**Sort the materials into magnetic,
non-magnetic and not sure.**

**Explain how you decided which
group each material should fit into.**

---

04 – MAGNETISM

Holding the object and the magnet,
slowly move them towards each other.

Describe what you can feel.

Why does this happen?

How is this used in everyday life?

---

05 – DIFFERENT MAGNETS

Examine the magnets.

How are they different?

How are the same?

Can you name any of the magnets?

---

06 – MAGNETISM

Holding the two magnets,
slowly move them towards each other.

Describe what you can feel.

Why does this happen?

**How does turning one of the magnets
around affect what happens? Why?**

Download a pdf of these activity cards from our website:
pstt.org.uk/eee-resources

CHALLENGING MISCONCEPTIONS:

1) The biggest magnet will be the strongest.

2) All metals are magnetic.

3) Smooth surfaces produce no friction.

1) The strength of a magnet is determined by the material it is made of and the strength of the external magnetic field applied when it was magnetised.

- Ask children to devise a simple test to investigate the strength of a magnet. (There are many possible tests – how many books will a magnet work through, how many paper clips will a magnet pick up, from how far away will a magnet attract a paperclip?) Which magnet was the strongest? Which magnet was the weakest? Was the biggest magnet the strongest? Was the smallest magnet the weakest?

2) Magnetic materials are always made of metal, but not all metals are magnetic. Iron, steel (an alloy of iron and carbon), nickel and cobalt are magnetic. Most other metals, for example aluminium, copper and gold, are NOT magnetic.

- In groups ask children to choose ten different materials/objects – five they think are magnetic and five they think are not. Discuss choices and reasons for them. Allow them to test them using a magnet. What do they notice?

- Compare aluminium and steel drink cans – what is the same, what is different? Test with a magnet. What happens? Why?

- Sort coins with a magnet. What do children notice? Why are some one pence, two pence, five pence and ten pence coins magnetic and some not?

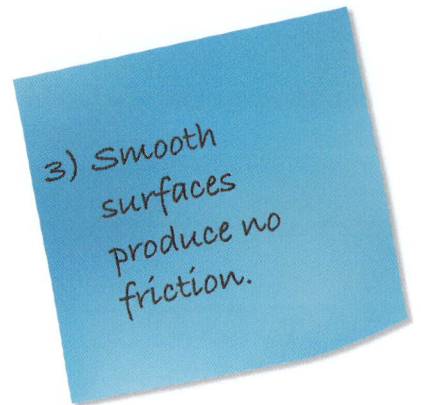

3) Friction occurs between all surfaces and materials including air and water. Rougher surfaces produce more friction, but even very smooth surfaces such as ice produce some friction.

- Measure the friction between an object and a surface by pulling the object across the surface using a force meter. Compare different surfaces, including oiled surfaces and ice. Even with very smooth surfaces there will be visible 'pull back' as the object resists movement due to friction.

QUESTIONS CHILDREN MAY ASK:

1) Why are objects attracted to the ends of magnets?

2) Why do rough surfaces stop things moving?

3) Why do magnets push each other?

1) The poles of a magnet are where the magnetic force is strongest. Bar magnets and horseshoe magnets have poles at each end. The poles of ring and button magnets are usually located on the flat circular faces.

• Observe a bar magnet's magnetic field by placing it underneath a clear plastic sheet, such as a box lid, and sprinkling on a handful of paper clips. What do children notice? Ensure children look from above and from the side – the magnetic field is 3D.

2) Rough surfaces have more irregularities – pits and bumps – and these will rub against each other as two materials move, snagging and catching and slowing the movement. Smooth surfaces have fewer irregularities so are usually easier to move across.

• Model the pits and bumps of rough surfaces using egg boxes. Try pulling one over another with spikes facing each other. Now turn one over and pull the smooth side over the spikes.

• Observe different materials using a microscope. What does the surface look like when magnified?

• Investigate the effects of lubricants – compare surfaces with and without lubricant. What do rough surfaces look like under the microscope once oil has been applied? How does this affect the amount of friction produced? Research applications of lubricant in everyday life.

3) All magnets have a north and a south pole. This is because magnetism is created by rotating charged particles (electrons) in atoms. Most of the electrons in an atom exist in pairs that spin in opposite directions, so the magnetic effect of one electron in a pair cancels out the effect of its partner. But if an atom has some unpaired electrons (iron atoms have four), these produce magnetic fields that line up with one another; this happens throughout the material and so it becomes a magnet. The direction of the magnetic field created is from the north pole to the south pole of the magnet.

• Model this using children to represent the flow of electricity. For north-north, children exit both magnets and bump off one another. For south-south, children enter the magnets moving away from each other. For north-south, children exit one magnet (north pole) and enter the other (south pole).

01 – PUSHES AND PULLS

why & how?

Examine the cards.

Talk about what is happening in each card.

Sort the cards into pushes, pulls, both and not sure.

Can you think of another example for each category?

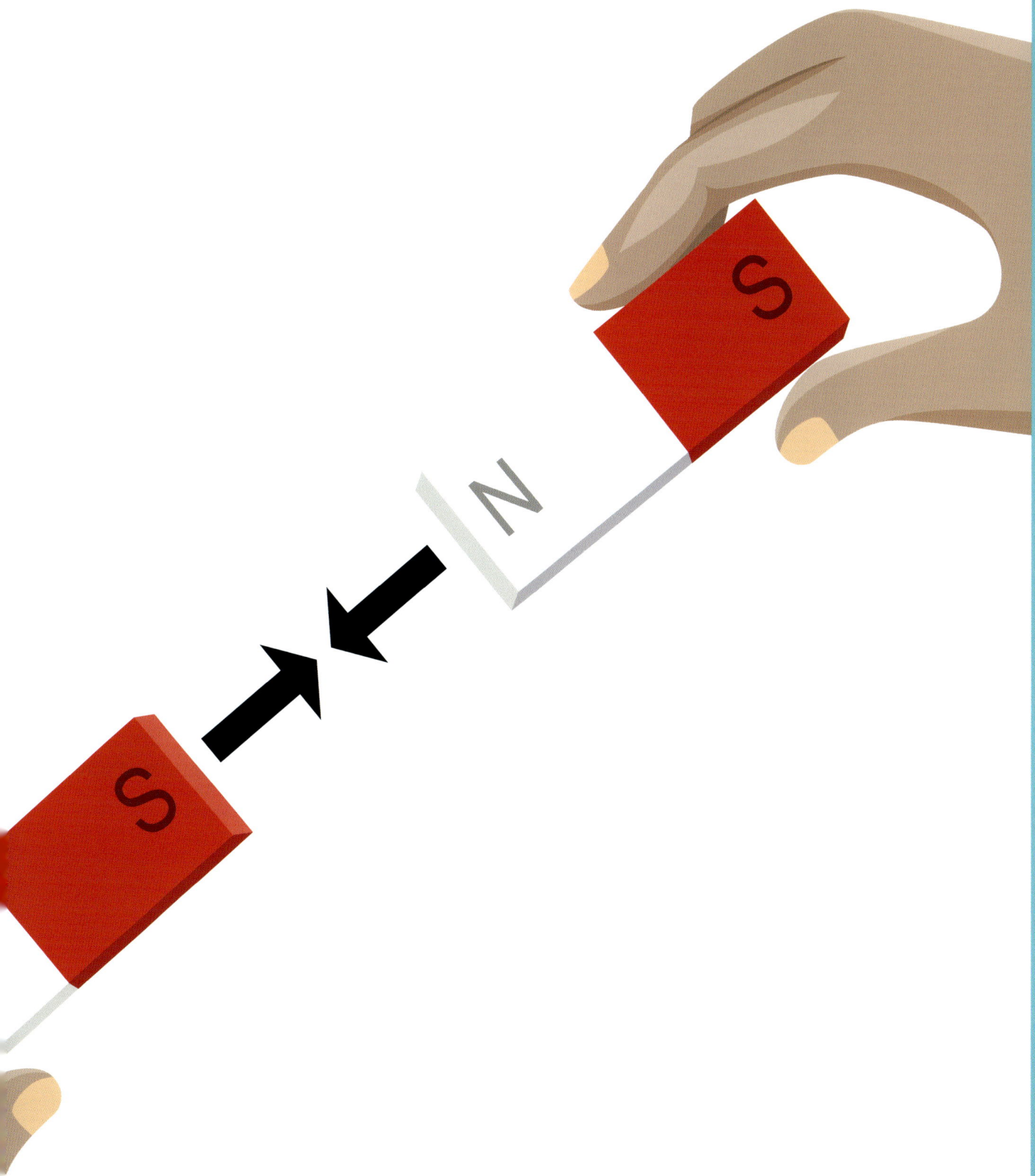

LIVING THINGS AND THEIR HABITATS

Key concepts

- Species depend on one another and their environment to survive.

- Living things can be grouped in a variety of ways.

- Classification keys can be used to help group, identify and name a variety of living things in the local and wider environment.

- Environments can change and this can sometimes pose dangers to living things.

Key vocabulary:

Classification	Fish	Vertebrate
Key	Amphibian	Invertebrate
Habitat	Reptile	Shelter
Environment	Bird	Food
Human impact	Mammal	Protection

Activity	Resources required	Background knowledge	What to look out for
01	Resource Sheet LIVING THINGS AND THEIR HABITATS 1	Every plant or animal lives in a habitat. A habitat is another name for a local environment. Seashores, gardens and ponds are all examples of habitats. Habitats can be big (a jungle, for example) or small (a leaf, for example). A habitat is a place where a collection of plants and animals live that provides them with what they need to survive.	Do children understand that plants and animals are suited to their environment – their habitat provides them with all the food, shelter and protection they need?
02	Resource Sheet LIVING THINGS AND THEIR HABITATS 2 or a photo of a local habitat.	Habitats should be explored using all the senses. Equipment needed includes specimen pots, magnifying lenses, identification keys, data loggers, sheets and nets.	Are children considering both animal life and plant life?
03	Two wild flowers from local area. Wildflower identification key.	Wildflowers can be identified in a number of ways, e.g. using leaf shape, colour and size, overall size of the plant, the month within which the plant bears flowers, petal shape, colour and size.	Which features are the children confidently describing? Can children use an identification key?
04	Resource Sheet LIVING THINGS AND THEIR HABITATS 4	Living things can be divided into groups by looking at similarities and differences between them. Plants are divided into flowering plants and non-flowering plants. Animals are divided into those that have a backbone (called vertebrates) and those that don't have a backbone (called invertebrates). Vertebrates and invertebrates are divided into smaller groups. Vertebrates are divided into five groups: fish, amphibians, reptiles, birds and mammals. Invertebrates are divided into six main groups: sponges, jellyfish, flatworms, roundworms, molluscs (include snail, slug, squid and octopus) and arthropods (include spiders, crustaceans and insects).'	Do children understand that the word 'animals' applies to all vertebrates and invertebrates and not just land animals? Are children using the words 'reptiles', 'amphibians', 'birds', 'fish', 'mammals', 'invertebrates'?
05	Resource Sheet LIVING THINGS AND THEIR HABITATS 5 or a photograph of a local habitat.	Seasonal changes to a habitat include the change from hot weather in the summer to cold weather in the winter, and the change from long hours of daylight in the summer to shorter days in the winter. The appearance of plant and animal life will alter accordingly. Over longer periods of time, species can disappear and new species take their place. Actions of humans can change a habitat.	Due to their limited lifespans so far, children may be unaware of how habitats can change over longer periods of time and how human action can have an impact on wildlife.
06	Resource Sheet LIVING THINGS AND THEIR HABITATS 6 or a photograph of a local park.	Many different species of plants and animals can be found in parks. Humans can help wildlife by leaving wildlife in the wild, sticking to paths, keeping dogs on leads, picking up rubbish, keeping noise levels low, and keeping a distance from animals. Humans can harm wildlife by littering, picking plants and touching animals, shouting, trampling over plants, allowing dogs to chase animals, and putting up buildings.	Are children aware of how the actions of humans impact wildlife – both plants and animals?

LESSON ACTIVITY CARDS:

YEAR 4 — LIVING THINGS AND THEIR HABITATS
01 – ANIMALS IN HABITATS

why & how?

Look carefully at the pictures.

Can you name each animal and match it to its habitat?

Describe each habitat – think about light, water, temperature, etc.

Why does each animal live where it does?
What else might you find living there?

YEAR 4 — LIVING THINGS AND THEIR HABITATS
02 – EXPLORING HABITATS

why & how?

Look at the picture.

What can you see?

How would you find out exactly what is living there?

What equipment would you need?

YEAR 4 — LIVING THINGS AND THEIR HABITATS
03 – WILDFLOWERS

why & how?

Observe the plants.

Describe each one.

How are they different and how are they the same?

How might you find out their names?
Can you use the key to identify each one?

YEAR 4 — LIVING THINGS AND THEIR HABITATS
04 – GROUPING ANIMALS

why & how?

Look at the animals on the cards.

What animals can you name?

**Can you group similar animals together?
What heading would each group have?**

Could you group them in a different way?
What heading would each group have now?

YEAR 4 — LIVING THINGS AND THEIR HABITATS
05 – CHANGES IN HABITATS

why & how?

Look at the picture.

What can you see?

How might this change over a year?

How might this change
over twenty years?

YEAR 4 — LIVING THINGS AND THEIR HABITATS
06 – HUMAN IMPACT

why & how?

Look at this picture carefully.

What might live in this park?

**How might humans help
living things in this park?**

How might humans disturb
living things in this park?

Download a pdf of these activity cards from our website:
pstt.org.uk/eee-resources

CHALLENGING MISCONCEPTIONS:

1) Animals and plants adapt to the environment they are in.

2) Spiders are insects.

3) Animals live on land.

1) Children tend to assume that plants and animals make the best of whatever environment they find themselves in. However, plants and animals are found in a particular habitat because they are suited to living there and only plants and animals with features and behaviour that suit the environment are able to survive.

- Children could create a choice chamber for woodlice to investigate which conditions they are suited to. Factors to change are light, temperature, dryness/dampness, shelter.

- One species of plant could be grown in a range of places with a variety of different conditions – light/dark, damp/dry, cold/warm – in order to see where it is most suited.

2) The word insect is used in everyday life to describe any invertebrate from slugs and snails to centipedes and spiders. The teacher will need to ensure children understand that insects have three major body parts – head, thorax and abdomen – and three pairs of legs. Most adult insects have wings. Spiders are arachnids, centipedes are myriapods, slugs and snails are molluscs. 'Invertebrates' is a better word to describe all these animals. Some teachers use 'minibeasts' as a group name for them.

- Reinforce correct use of vocabulary by playing 'Simon Says' with a twist. Teacher to call out an invertebrate name. e.g. 'Simon loves...spiders.' Children should move like the invertebrate unless it is an insect. Children won't get to fly – make sure they notice that all flying invertebrates are insects; however, not all insects can fly.

- Compare and contrast an ant and a spider, using questions to focus observations. What is the same? What is different? How many major body parts does each have? How many legs? (Observations of real invertebrates are preferable to studying pictures if possible.)

- Children could design their own insect. How many major body parts and legs should they have?

- Go on a bug hunt. Children could record findings as 'Insects' and 'Other invertebrates' and compare findings in different areas of the school grounds or local environment.

3) The word 'animal' describes all vertebrates and invertebrates including birds, fish, amphibians, reptiles, mammals and invertebrates and not just those found on land.

- Create a classification key using a frame and the terms above – animal, vertebrate, invertebrate, birds, fish, reptiles, amphibians, mammals, insects. This can be done as a class, discussing which term should go where and why, or as groups, allowing children to research/look up words and then compare/discuss each group's key as a class.

QUESTIONS CHILDREN MAY ASK:

1) Do all living things in the same habitat have things in common?

2) Why do animals have different features?

3) What do dragonflies, centipedes, worms, etc. eat?

1) Each habitat contains a wide variety of animals and plants that depend on one another and their environment to survive.

- Survey a habitat. Each group of children could survey a different habitat in the school grounds or local area. What plants and animals can you find in 1 m²? Use an identification key to identify plants. For animals, use nets to sweep long grasses, sheets to shake shrubs, hedges and trees onto. Record via photos or annotated sketches. Each group of children could survey a different habitat in the school grounds or local area. Use evidence to answer the question. What would happen if all animals in one habitat were all the same? What would happen if all the plants were the same?

2) Animals have different features according to where they live, what they eat and how they behave.

- Adaptation is usually covered later on in primary schooling. Stick with researching invertebrate differences and the reasons for these, e.g. Why do snails have shells but centipedes do not? Why do spiders spin webs? Why do woodlice have an exoskeleton? How do these features help the animal survive?

3) Children may each want to know a lot of information about different animals in a habitat, e.g. what they eat, where they live, how long they live for and how they reproduce.

- It would be impossible to cover each animal in which they are interested, as a class; however, children could research their own animal and produce a 'Top Trumps' or 'Deadly 60' – style fact card and create rules on how to use them in a game.

01 – ANIMALS IN HABITATS

YEAR 4
LIVING THINGS AND THEIR HABITATS:
01 – ANIMALS IN HABITATS

why&
how?

Look carefully at the pictures.

**Can you name each animal
and match it to its habitat?**

**Describe each habitat – think about light,
water, temperature, etc.**

**Why does each animal live where it does?
What else might you find living there?**

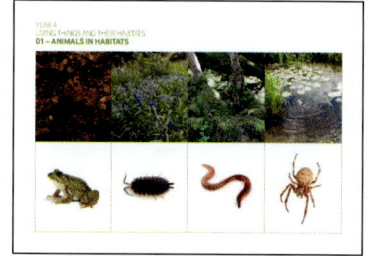

02 – EXPLORING HABITATS

YEAR 4
LIVING THINGS AND THEIR HABITATS:
02 – EXPLORING HABITATS

why&
how?

Look at the picture.

What can you see?

**How would you find out
exactly what is living there?**

What equipment would you need?

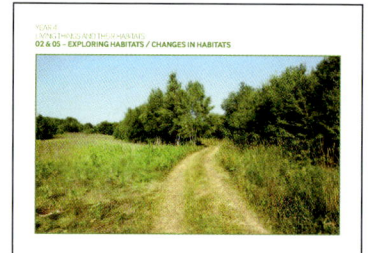

04 – GROUPING ANIMALS

YEAR 4
LIVING THINGS AND THEIR HABITATS:
04 – GROUPING ANIMALS

why&
how?

Look at the animals on the cards.

What animals can you name?

Can you group similar animals together?
What heading would each group have?

Could you group them in a different way?
What heading would each group have now?

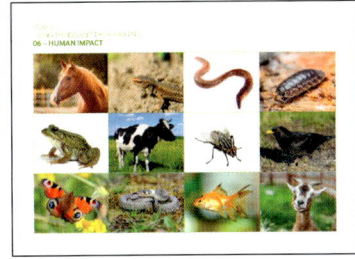

06 – HUMAN IMPACT

05 – CHANGES IN HABITATS

why&
how?

Look at the picture.

What can you see?

How might this change over a year?

**How might this change
over twenty years?**

YEAR 4
LIVING THINGS AND THEIR HABITATS:
02 & 05 – EXPLORING HABITATS / CHANGES IN HABITATS

06 – HUMAN IMPACT

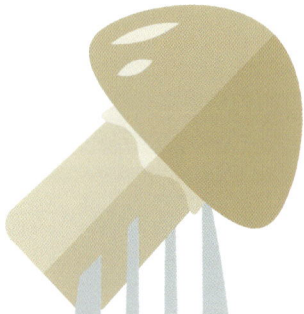

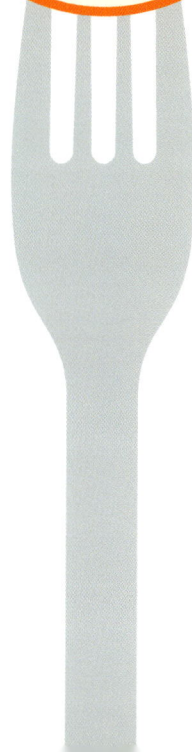

ANIMALS, INCLUDING HUMANS – TEETH AND EATING

Key concepts

- The digestive system in humans is comprised of several parts and each has a special function.

- Teeth in animals differ according to their natural diet.

- Teeth can be damaged and need to be cared for.

- Living things rely on each other for food in the natural world; food chains and food webs can illustrate this relationship.

Key vocabulary:

Digestive system	Pre-molar	Oesophagus	Omnivore
Nutrition	Saliva	Stomach	Producer
Nutrients	Tongue	Small intestine	Consumer
Mouth	Rip	Large intestine	Predator
Teeth	Tear	Rectum	Prey
Canine	Chew	Anus	Food chain
Incisor	Grind	Carnivore	
Molar	Cut	Herbivore	

Year 4 – Animals, Including Humans – Teeth and Eating

Activity	Resources required	Background knowledge	What to look out for
01	Resource sheet TEETH AND EATING 1	The main body parts associated with the digestive system are the mouth, tongue, teeth, oesophagus, stomach, small and large intestine and rectum. Each has a special part to play in breaking down and absorbing food so our body can use the nutrients.	Which parts of our digestive system can they draw and name?
02	Teeth – incisors, molars, canines and pre-molars. Real examples or models children can handle are preferable to pictures.	There are four different tooth types in humans and each has a slightly different shape and performs a different function. Incisors have a sharp biting surface and are used for cutting or shearing food into small chewable pieces. Canines have a sharp, pointed biting surface. Their function is to grip and tear food. Pre-molars and molars (molars look similar but are larger than pre-molars) have flat biting surfaces to chew, crush and grind food.	Do children know the names of any teeth? Can they explain why they are different, referring to diet and not just size and animal of origin?
03	Resource sheet TEETH AND EATING 3	Sugary foods and drinks are harmful to our teeth. Our mouths are full of bacteria and some of these feed on the sugars eaten. This creates an acid that starts to dissolve the enamel – the hard, shiny outer layer of a tooth. If it continues, the tooth can develop a hole (called a cavity) where the inside of the tooth rots – this can cause toothache. Foods that are good for our teeth are dairy products, salmon, leafy green vegetables and crunchy vegetables such as carrots, or fruit such as apples (although these are acidic, which is not good for enamel).	Are children clear about the difference between 'good for our teeth' and 'good for our body'? Can they name foods and drinks that are beneficial for our teeth?
04	Resource sheet TEETH AND EATING 4	Plant eaters are herbivores, meat eaters are carnivores, and animals that eat both plants and animals are omnivores	Can children sort animals accurately? If not, are they confused by the vocabulary or unsure of the animals' diets?
05	Resource sheet TEETH AND EATING 5	All living things need food for survival. Animals get energy and nutrients by eating other animals or plants. These links between animals and plants are called food chains. Nearly all food chains start with a green plant. Plants are called producers because they make their own food. Plants get their energy from the Sun. Animals are called consumers because they eat other plants and animals.	Can children link living things into a simple food chain? Do they understand that the arrows mean 'is eaten by'?
06	Resource sheet TEETH AND EATING 6	A predator is an animal that eats other animals. The animals that predators eat are called prey. Animals can be both predators and prey.	Can children sort animals accurately? If not, are they confused by the vocabulary or unsure of the animals' diets?

LESSON ACTIVITY CARDS:

YEAR 4
ANIMALS, INCLUDING HUMANS – TEETH AND EATING
01 – DIGESTIVE SYSTEM

Food travels through your body.

Draw the body parts your food travels through on the body outline.

Can you name each part?

What does each part do?

YEAR 4
ANIMALS, INCLUDING HUMANS – TEETH AND EATING
02 – EXAMINING TEETH

Food travels through your body.

**What is the same about them?
What is different?**

Can you name any different types of teeth?

Why are teeth shaped differently?

YEAR 4
ANIMALS, INCLUDING HUMANS – TEETH AND EATING
03 – CARING FOR TEETH

How should we take care of our teeth?

Can you sort the food and drinks into those that are bad for our teeth, good for our teeth and neither good nor bad?

How do food and drink damage teeth?

YEAR 4
ANIMALS, INCLUDING HUMANS – TEETH AND EATING
04 – ANIMAL DIET

Examine the animal cards.

Can you sort the animals into carnivores, herbivores and omnivores?

What does each word mean?

Can you think of another animal for each group?

YEAR 4
ANIMALS, INCLUDING HUMANS – TEETH AND EATING
05 – CREATING FOOD CHAINS

Examine the cards.

Can you make a simple food chain using all or some of the cards?

What do the arrows mean?

How is the Sun involved in all food chains?

YEAR 4
ANIMALS, INCLUDING HUMANS – TEETH AND EATING
06 – USING FOOD CHAIN VOCABULARY

Examine the cards.

Can you sort the animals into predators, prey and both?

What do the words 'predator' and 'prey' mean?

Can you think of another animal for each group?

Download a pdf of these activity cards from our website:
pstt.org.uk/eee-resources

CHALLENGING MISCONCEPTIONS:

1) When you eat, food goes down one tube and drink goes down another.

2) Your food is digested in your stomach.

3) Cheese is bad for your teeth as it contains too much fat.

1) Children think food and drink travel down different tubes to your stomach. However both travel to your stomach via the oesophagus.

- Ask children to place hands either side of their throat as they eat and drink. What can they feel? Does it feel different when swallowing food and drink?

- Show children an X-ray of a human eating and drinking.

- Use Virtuali-Tee Educational Augmented Reality t-shirt or virtual digestive system apps such as Anatomy 4D to explore the components of our digestive system. Create your own digestive system t-shirts using fabric pens on plain t-shirts or felt tips on a paper tabard.

2) Children do not recognise the part that teeth and saliva play in breaking down food.

- Model the action of the stomach with transparent food bags. In one, place a crunched up biscuit mixed with a little saliva (water), this has been 'chewed'. In the other, put a whole biscuit. Add stomach acid (lemon juice) to both bags and squeeze and crush both bags to represent the action of the stomach muscles. Which biscuit breaks down first? Why? Why are our teeth and saliva an important part of the digestive system? We eat as we need the nutrients from our food – protein, carbohydrates, fat, vitamins, minerals. We can only use nutrients that have been broken down and dissolved. Food is broken down into smaller pieces by chewing. The teeth cut and crush the food, while it's mixed with saliva. Saliva contains enzymes, which begin breaking down parts of the food. This process helps to make it soft, easier to swallow and easier for the stomach to continue breaking down the pieces.

3) Children confuse 'bad for health' and 'bad for teeth'. Foods that are bad for our general health are high in fat, salt or sugar. Foods that are bad for our teeth are high in acid or sugar.

- Research how the body uses sugar, fat, salt and acids. Which are useful and why? Which are harmful and why? Children could research one component in pairs and create some TRUE or FALSE facts to ask the rest of the class. Hold TRUE or FALSE quiz as a class.

QUESTIONS CHILDREN MAY ASK:

1) How does sugar rot your teeth?

2) What are our teeth made of?
Why do we need to use a toothbrush?

3) Where does our food go when we swallow it?

1) Bacteria feed on sugar left on your teeth and produce acid, which dissolves enamel.

- Children could compare the sugar content and acidity of a range of soft drinks (pH test). A simple comparative test can be set up by placing egg shell in samples of the drinks, leaving for a few days and then observing changes to the surface of the shell.

2) Teeth are comprised of three main layers – pulp with blood supply and nerves, dentine and enamel.

- Children could research the parts of a tooth and recreate a cross-section using coloured playdough.
- Children could use teeth models to investigate how effective toothbrushes are compared to rinsing or using cloths or other utensils. Use permanent pen or similar to represent food and drink residue, use each method for two minutes and compare results.

3) Food travels down the oesophagus to the stomach, then through the small and large intestines with the waste moving on to the rectum and out via the anus.

- Children could choose everyday utensils to represent each key part of our digestive system. Using the utensils, 'digest' a banana and/or biscuit. Each step should be evaluated – how effective was their choice?

01 – DIGESTIVE SYSTEM

YEAR 4
ANIMALS, INCLUDING HUMANS – TEETH AND EATING:
01 – DIGESTIVE SYSTEM

why & how?

Food travels through your body.

Draw the body parts your food travels through on the body outline.

Can you name each part?

What does each part do?

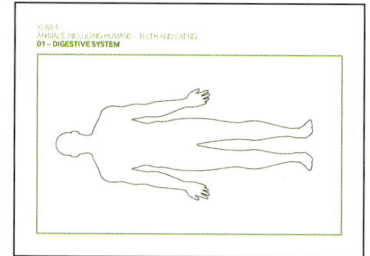

03 – CARING FOR TEETH

YEAR 4
ANIMALS, INCLUDING HUMANS – TEETH AND EATING:
03 – CARING FOR TEETH

why & how?

How should we take care of our teeth?

Can you sort the food and drinks into those that are bad for our teeth, good for our teeth and neither good nor bad?

How do food and drink damage teeth?

04 – ANIMAL DIET

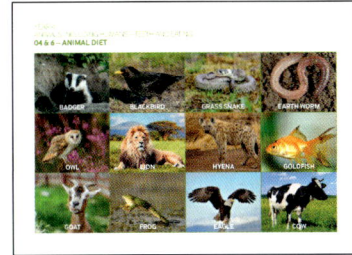

05 – CREATING FOOD CHAINS

YEAR 4
ANIMALS, INCLUDING HUMANS – TEETH AND EATING:
05 – CREATING FOOD CHAINS

why & how?

Examine the cards.

Can you make a simple food chain using all or some of the cards?

What do the arrows mean?

How is the Sun involved in all food chains?

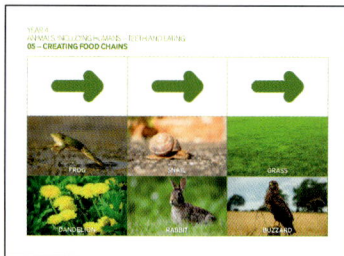

06 – USING FOOD CHAIN VOCABULARY

YEAR 4
ANIMALS, INCLUDING HUMANS – TEETH AND EATING:
06 – USING FOOD CHAIN VOCABULARY

why&
how?

Examine the cards.

**Can you sort the animals into
predators, prey and both?**

What do the words 'predator' and 'prey' mean?

**Can you think of another
animal for each group?**

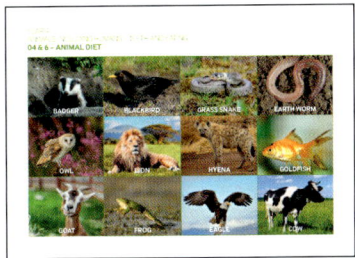

04 & 6 – ANIMAL DIET

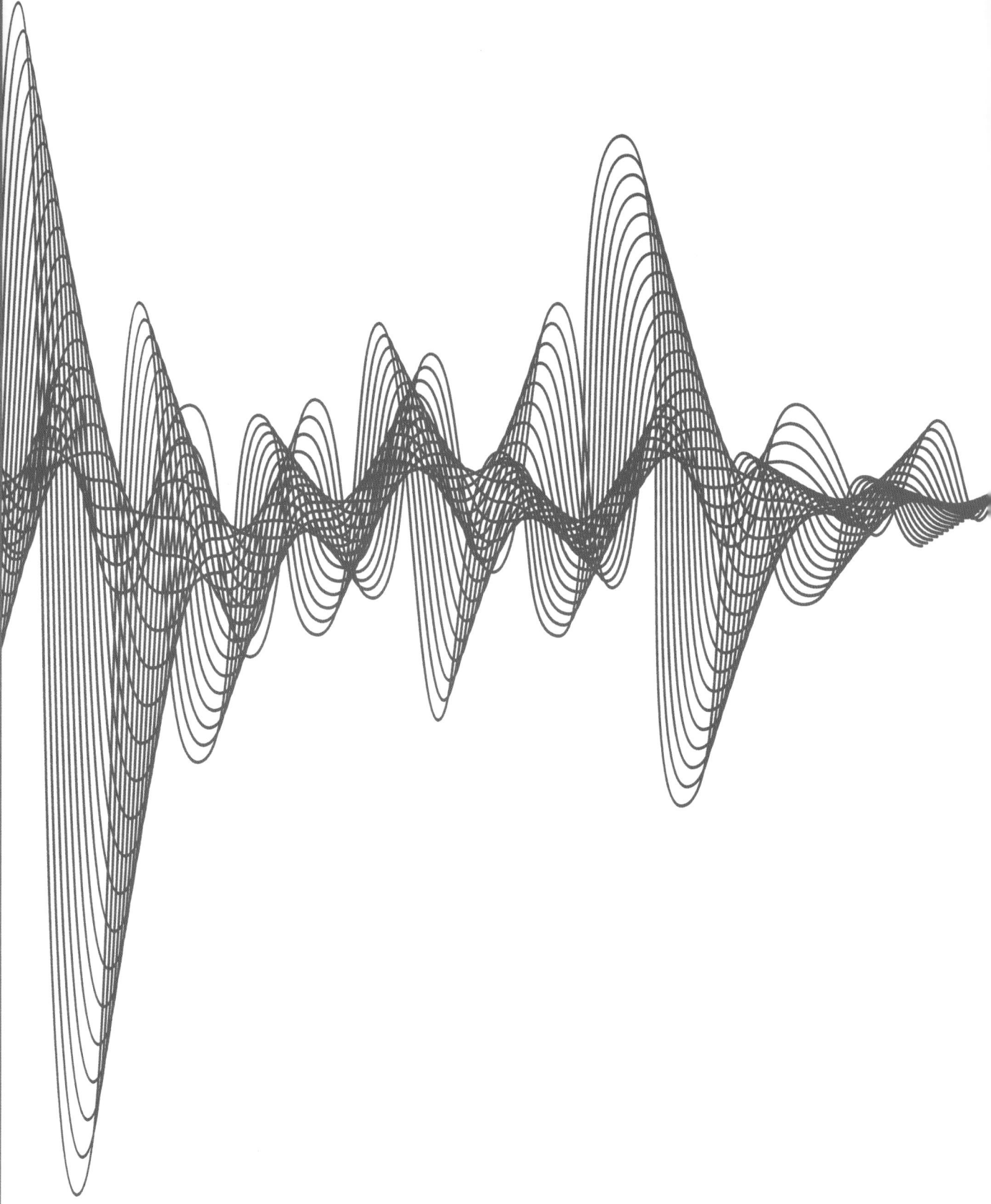

SOUND

Key concepts

- Sounds are made by something vibrating.

- Vibrations from sounds travel through a medium (solids, liquids, gases) to the ear.

- The pitch of a sound depends on the features of the object that produced it.

- The volume of a sound depends on the strength of the vibrations that produced it.

- Sounds get fainter as the distance from the sound source increases.

Key vocabulary:

Sound	Gas	Insulation
Source	Pitch	Instrument
Noise	High	Percussion
Vibrate	Low	Strings
Vibration	Volume	Brass
Travel	Loud	Woodwind
Solid	Quiet	Tune
Liquid	Fainter	

Activity	Resources required	Background knowledge	What to look out for
01	A drum, a drum stick and some rice.	Hitting the drum causes the skin to vibrate and the rice to jump. The harder the drum is hit, the bigger the vibration, the louder the sound and the higher the rice jumps. The softer the drum is hit, the smaller the vibration, the quieter the sound and the lower the rice jumps.	Are children using words such as louder/quieter? Do children associate the jumping rice with the vibrating skin, or do they link it directly with the drum stick action?
02	Inflated balloons. *Warning – children may suffer from a latex allergy.	Children's voices cause vibrations, which travel through the air to the balloon, through the balloon to the air inside the balloon, back through the other side of the balloon, through the air again and into their partner's ear.	Do children use the words 'vibrate/vibrations'? Do children know what is causing the vibrations?
03	None needed.	Sounds get fainter as the distance from the source increases. Sounds coming from the left will reach our left ear very slightly before our right ear and vice versa. Our ears and brain detect differences in the timing and volume of sounds to help us create a 3D 'sound picture' and accurately place sources of sounds.	Are children using words such as 'louder/quieter'? Do children notice that the sound is fainter as the distance increases?
04	Plastic tub or box, elastic bands of different widths and lengths.	Four different factors affect pitch: tension (loose/tight), diameter (thick/thin), length (short/long) and density (e.g. copper v steel). Sounds of low pitch will be produced by thick, loose or long elastic bands. Sounds of high pitch will be produced by thin, tight or short elastic bands.	Are children using the words 'high', 'low' and 'pitch'? Can they spot a pattern in the features of the elastic bands and the sounds made?
05	Six different glass bottles with a different amount of liquid in each. Something metal to tap the bottles with.	When you hit the bottle with the spoon, the glass vibrates and these vibrations make the sound. Tapping an empty bottle produces a higher-pitched sound than tapping a bottle full of water. Adding water to the bottle dampens the vibrations created by striking the glass with a spoon. The less water in the bottle, the faster the glass vibrates and the higher the pitch. The more water in the bottle, the slower the glass vibrates, creating a lower pitch.	Are children using the words 'high', 'low' and 'pitch'? Can they spot a pattern in the amount of water and the sounds made? Do children know what is causing the sound?
06	A metal cooling rack or coat hanger with 50cm of string tied to two corners. Something metal to tap the rack/hanger with.	Sound can travel through solids, liquids and gases; however, sound travels differently through each of these media. When we listen to the coat hanger through the string tied to it, the vibrations travel to our ears through the string, not through air. This creates a more direct path and lets more of the sound reach your ears, which is why it sounds different.	Are children using the words 'vibrate/vibration', 'low/high', 'loud/quiet'? Are children talking about sound travelling through different media?

LESSON ACTIVITY CARDS:

YEAR 4 SOUND
01 – JUMPING RICE
why & how?

Sprinkle some rice on the drum.
Tap the drum gently with the drum stick.

What happens to the rice?

Can you change how high the rice jumps? How?

What does this tell you about how sounds are created?

YEAR 4 SOUND
02 – BALLOON
why & how?

Hold the balloon up to your partner's ear.
Put your lips gently up against the other side of the balloon and talk quietly to your partner.

What does he/she feel? Where does he/she feel it?

What happens if you speak loudly/quietly?

What is causing this?

YEAR 4 SOUND
03 – LOCATING SOUND SOURCE
why & how?

Work with a partner. Close your eyes.
Your partner should say your name quietly while standing in different places.

Can you tell where your partner is standing?

How does the sound change as she/he moves?

What else might affect how a sound is heard?

YEAR 4 SOUND
04 – CHANGING SOUNDS WITH ELASTIC BANDS
why & how?

Stretch the elastic bands over the tub.

What happens when you pluck them?

Do they all make the same sound?

How could you change the sound they make?

YEAR 4 SOUND
05 – CHANGING SOUNDS WITH WATER
why & how?

Gently tap the bottles.

Can you put them in order of highest to lowest sound?

Why are the sounds different?

How is the sound being made?

YEAR 4 SOUND
06 – SOUND AND MEDIA
why & how?

Hold the metal rack by the string, looping the ends around each index finger. Ask your partner to hit the rack gently with the metal spoon.

What happens? What can you feel? What can you hear?

Can you change the sound?

Stick your fingers in your ears and lean forward so the rack does not touch you.
Ask your partner to hit the rack gently again.

What can you feel and hear now? Why is there a difference?

Download a pdf of these activity cards from our website:
pstt.org.uk/eee-resources

CHALLENGING MISCONCEPTIONS:

1) Sound travels through air better than solids and liquids because it is thinner.

2) Wider elastic bands make a louder sound.

3) When I hit the drum harder it makes a higher sound.

1) Children think sound cannot travel through solids and liquids or that it travels better through air.

- Use string telephones to compare how sound travels through solids and air by talking to a partner standing at a distance with and without the telephone. Does the distance and length of string make a difference? Could a different material be used in place of string – e.g. metal or plastic wire, elastic?

- Make a hydrophone by carefully cutting the bottom off a plastic bottle. Place the bottle cut-side down in a bowl of water and put your ear up against the hole at the top. Ask a partner to gently tap spoons and other hard objects together under the water. What do you hear? How does it compare to the sounds heard if the same is repeated without the water?

2+3) Children confuse the vocabulary used for pitch and volume.

- Use a data logger to visually demonstrate the difference between loud sounds and quiet sounds. Repeat to show that volume does not change with pitch.

- Show how size (loudness/volume) or speed (pitch) of vibrations change using salt/sugar on baking parchment stretched over a glass bowl and secured with an elastic band. Place a portable Bluetooth speaker inside the bowl and play notes of different volume or pitch via laptop/tablet. Compare the movement of the particles.

QUESTIONS CHILDREN MAY ASK:

1) Why does the rice jump up and down on the drum?

2) Why do some drums make low sounds and some drums make high sounds.

3) How do our ears help us to hear?

1) All sounds are caused by vibrations. There are lots of demonstrations involving careful observation to show that sound is caused by vibrations and that is what causes the rice to jump up and down:

- Children can place their fingertips on their throat and speak. What can they feel? How does this change if they speak quietly/loudly or change the note?

- Show how a tuning fork causes sound against a table top, and then repeat but place the tongs of the fork into a dish of water once struck.

- Twang a ruler placed half on and half off a table. Move the ruler further on/off the table. How do the vibrations change? How does the sound change?

2) Investigate changes in pitch and volume using instruments.

- Use stringed instruments to investigate and observe how the thickness of the string, the tightness of the string and the length of the string can change the pitch of the note. Can children spot a pattern between the thickness of the string and the sound produced? What about the tightness of the string and the sound produced? What about the length of the string and the sound produced?

- Repeat with other types of instrument. In each case, what is vibrating and how is it vibrating, i.e. quickly, slowly, strongly, gently? How can the sound being produced be changed?

- Children could reinforce their understanding by creating their own instruments from paper straws, bamboo, elastic bands, bottles, etc. Instruments should be able to produce sounds of different pitch and volume.

3) Looking at the shape and size of our outer ear, its function and how it compares to other animals, makes an interesting investigation. Our outer ears act as funnels – collecting and directing sound to our inner ear.

- Children could design and test their own ear-like "hearing aids," looking at animal ears for clues about what helps improve the auditory sense.

- Research animals with excellent hearing – how big are their ears, what shape are they and where are they situated? Why is good hearing important to them?

- Do bigger ears make you hear better? Does the shape of the ear matter? Children can make add-on 'ears' out of paper plates. Which size works best? What shape improves hearing the most? How does changing the angle alter what can be heard?

ELECTRICITY – CIRCUITS AND CONDUCTORS

Key concepts

- An electric circuit is a continuous loop of conducting materials.

- A complete, closed circuit is needed for electricity to flow.

- The basic components of an electrical circuit are cells, wires, bulbs, switches and buzzers.

- A switch opens and closes a circuit.

- Some materials do not allow electricity to pass and these are called insulators.

- Some materials do allow electricity to pass and these are called conductors.

- Some common appliances run on electricity.

- Mains electricity can be dangerous.

Key vocabulary:

Electricity	Circuit symbol	Short circuit	Motor
Appliance	Component	Wire	Conductor
Device	Cell	Crocodile clip	Insulator
Mains	Battery	Bulb	Metal
Plug	Positive	Bright	Non metal
Electrical circuit	Negative	Dim	
Complete circuit	Connect	Switch	
Circuit diagram	Connection	Buzzer	

Activity	Resources required	Background knowledge	What to look out for
01	Simple circuit components. (Either just the correct components or make a moving object change direction, some extra parts and red herrings.)	A circuit always needs a power source, such as a battery, with wires connected to both the positive (+) and negative (-) ends. A battery is also known as a cell. A circuit can also contain other electrical components, such as bulbs, buzzers or motors, which allow electricity to pass through. The electrical energy can be converted into other types of energy such as light, heat, movement or sound.	Can children name the parts and build a working circuit? Are they using the words 'cell', 'wire', 'bulb'? Do they understand what each component does – even the wires?
02	Resource Sheet CIRCUITS AND CONDUCTORS 2	Electricity will only travel around a circuit that is complete – a continuous loop of conducting materials. That means it has no gaps. As soon as there is a gap/break in the circuit, electricity cannot flow.	Do children realise that a break in the circuit – whether an unconnected wire or open switch – will mean that the circuit is not complete and the bulb will not light?
03	A switch.	When a switch is open (off), there is a gap in the circuit. Electricity cannot travel around the circuit. When a switch is closed (on), it makes the circuit complete and electricity can travel around the circuit. Switches can be found on most appliances powered by electricity, e.g. light switches, TV on/off button, on/off button for mobile phones and tablets, electric sockets, etc.	Can children name the part? Do they know it opens or closes the circuit, and so either allows or does not allow the electricity to flow?
04	A range of materials – some conductors and some insulators.	Some materials let electricity pass through them easily. These materials are known as electrical conductors. Many metals, such as copper, iron and steel, are good electrical conductors. Some materials do not allow electricity to pass through them. These materials are known as electrical insulators. Plastic, wood, glass and rubber are good electrical insulators.	Do children know that metals are good conductors? Do they know the word 'insulator'?
05	Resource Sheet CIRCUITS AND CONDUCTORS 5	Many household items are powered by mains electricity or batteries. These include most watches, torches, calculators, central heating, etc.	Do children recognise that appliances that are 'plugged in' AND those using batteries are powered by electricity?
06	Resource Sheet CIRCUITS AND CONDUCTORS 6	Electricity is made at a power station and travels down large cables to people's houses. This electricity is known as mains power and is very dangerous. It can kill, so children should never play near it. Mains electricity is essentially a big circuit so, when you plug something in at home, you complete the circuit from your house to the power station and back again.	Can children come up with any rules to keep themselves safe around mains electricity?

LESSON ACTIVITY CARDS:

YEAR 4
ELECTRICITY – CIRCUITS AND CONDUCTORS
01 – PARTS OF A CIRCUIT

why
how?

Use the equipment to make a simple
circuit with a bulb that lights.

Can you name each component
of the circuit?

What does each component do?

YEAR 4
ELECTRICITY – CIRCUITS AND CONDUCTORS
02 – LIGHTING A BULB

why
how?

Look at the pictures of circuits.
In which circuits would the bulb be lit?

Why?

Why will the others not work?

YEAR 4
ELECTRICITY – CIRCUITS AND CONDUCTORS
03 – SWITCHES

why
how?

Look at the circuit component.
What is this component called?

What does it do?

Where can you find these
around your home?

YEAR 4
ELECTRICITY – CIRCUITS AND CONDUCTORS
04 – CONDUCTORS

why
how?

Look at the materials.
Can you name them?

Which ones will conduct electricity?

What do we call materials that
do not conduct electricity?

YEAR 4
ELECTRICITY – CIRCUITS AND CONDUCTORS
05 – MAINS AND BATTERIES

why
how?

Look at the appliances.
Can you name them?

Can you sort them into two groups – those
powered by electricity and those not?

Could we survive without electricity?
Why/why not?

YEAR 4
ELECTRICITY – CIRCUITS AND CONDUCTORS
06 – HAZARDS

why
how?

Look at this picture carefully.
What electrical hazards can
you spot in this picture?

Why are they hazardous?

Can you write three rules for
using mains electricity safely?

Download a pdf of these activity cards from our website:
pstt.org.uk/eee-resources

CHALLENGING MISCONCEPTIONS:

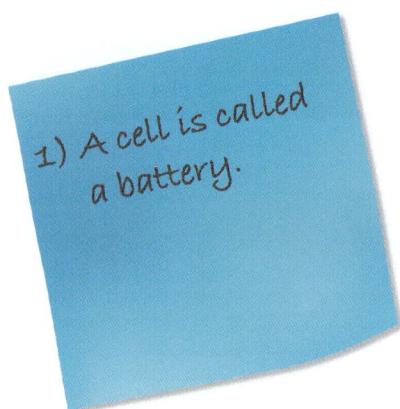

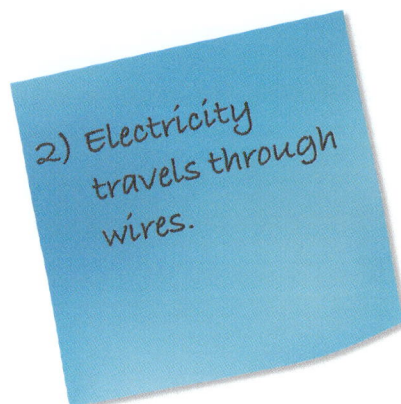

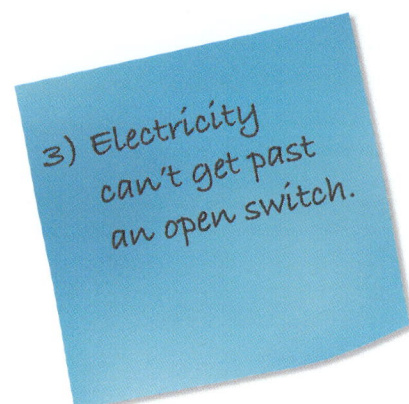

1) A cell is called a battery.

2) Electricity travels through wires.

3) Electricity can't get past an open switch.

1) A cell is a power supply that uses chemical energy to make electricity. A battery is made up of two or more cells connected in series. Due to the use of the term 'battery' to describe a cell in everyday life, both adults and children may misuse it in a science context.

• Play vocabulary games to reinforce correct scientific terminology for all circuit components. e.g.

Picture Bingo: Use pictures on the Bingo card and call out the scientific words that accurately name the pictures.

Taboo: Taking turns in teams, one team member has to describe a given component without using its name.

Word Acrostic: Write a word or phrase for each letter of the word – make this harder by requiring the words and phrases to be related to that word.

2+3) Children may see electricity as something that travels from the cell through 'empty' wires to the component and then away again, when in fact electric charges (electrons) are found throughout a circuit; these all move simultaneously and flow around the circuit to create a current due to the 'push' of the cell. All the electrons stop moving when the circuit is broken. Switches cause a break in a circuit.

• Use a rope loop analogy to illustrate that electrical charge is present throughout the circuit and the energy from the cell pushes the charge around the circuit – this is called a current. A circuit is modelled as a big loop of rope. One person is the cell and pushes the rope forwards while pulling the loop through their hands. Another person is the bulb and squeezes (resists) the rope. Friction with the hands of the resistor person means they can feel the energy transferred as heat. Ask children to complete sentences such as:

The pupil starting the movement is like the ... in the circuit.

The rope is like the... in the electric circuit.

The pupil gripping the rope is like the... in the electric circuit.

Just like the pupil's hands gripping the rope, the bulb provides a ...against the flow of the electric current.

What would happen if the rope was cut? What component would this be like?

• Use balls to represent charges. In this analogy everyone stands in a circle and holds a ball – the balls are electrical charge. To show the current flowing, each person passes their ball to the person next to them. This shows that the charges are already there and they move everywhere at the same time. One person can step back from the circle – opening a switch – this means that the flow cannot continue until the switch is closed and the person steps back in the circle.

QUESTIONS CHILDREN MAY ASK:

1) Why do some materials conduct electricity and some don't?

2) Why do TVs need to be plugged in?

3) Why do batteries stop working?

1) Only materials that contain electrical charge will conduct electricity.

- Refer back to the rope and ball analogies on the opposite page. What would happen if the rope had missing chunks? What if some children did not hold balls?

2) Mains electricity is made at a power station and travels down large cables to people's houses. Mains electricity is essentially a big circuit so, when you plug something in at home, you complete the circuit from your house to the power station and back again.

- Take apart electrical wiring, plugs and appliance connections to show children how electricity flows towards and from the appliance to the mains and to and from the mains to the appliance.

- Take apart a socket switch or light switch to investigate the mechanism – compare to the switch of a simple circuit.

- Compare components of a simple circuit to components of mains electricity. The power station provides electrical energy like a cell. Electrical charge flows along simple circuit wires and household electrical wires. Socket switches open and close the circuit just like a simple circuit switch. The television uses electrical energy, just like a bulb, buzzer or motor in a simple circuit.

- Children can create a diagram to illustrate a mains electricity circuit from a power station to a TV and back again.

3) Cells have chemicals inside, which react to create electrical energy. Once the chemicals have been used up, the battery can no longer produce electrical energy.

- Get children to run around the field and sit down once they are out of energy. Where does their energy come from? (Food they eat) How would they get more energy? (Eat more food) Compare to cells. Some cells can be recharged.

- Investigate the length of time cells that work for. Children to set up simple comparative tests around the question 'What affects how long a battery lasts for?' Use post-it note planning to explore ideas. These could include brand, cost, appliance being run, type of cell (AA, AAA, etc).

02 – LIGHTING A BULB

YEAR 4
ELECTRICITY – CIRCUITS AND CONDUCTORS:
02 – LIGHTING A BULB

why &
how?

Look at the pictures of circuits.

In which circuits would the bulb be lit?

Why?

Why will the others not work?

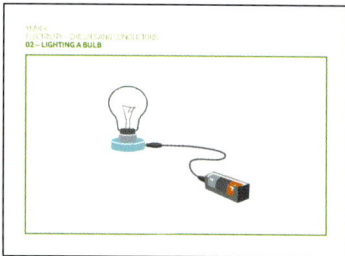

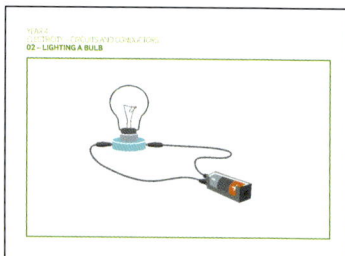

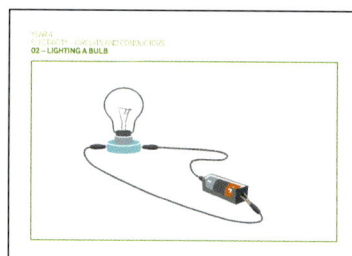

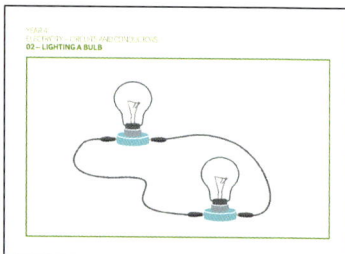

05 – MAINS AND BATTERIES

YEAR 4
ELECTRICITY – CIRCUITS AND CONDUCTORS:
05 – MAINS AND BATTERIES

why&
how?

Look at the appliances.

Can you name them?

Can you sort them into two groups – those powered by electricity and those not?

Could we survive without electricity? Why/why not?

06 – HAZARDS

YEAR 4
ELECTRICITY – CIRCUITS AND CONDUCTORS:
06 – HAZARDS

why&
how?

Look at this picture carefully.

What electrical hazards can you spot in this picture?

Why are they hazardous?

Can you write three rules for using mains electricity safely?

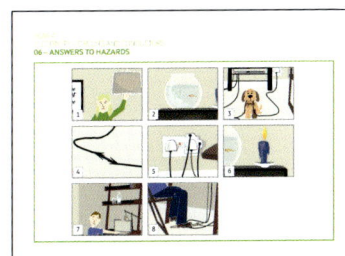

STATES OF MATTER

Key concepts

- Materials can be solids, liquids or gases.

- Materials change state with heating or cooling.

- The rates of evaporation and condensation are affected by temperature.

- Evaporation and condensation play a part in the water cycle where water circulates between the Earth's oceans, atmosphere and land.

Key vocabulary:

State	Steam	Solidify
Matter	Heated	Boil
Solid	Heat	Boiling point
Liquid	Cooled	Evaporate
Gas	Cool	Evaporation
Air	Temperature	Condense
Oxygen	Degrees Celsius	Condensation
Ice	Melt	Water cycle
Water	Melting point	Precipitation
Water vapour	Freeze	Infiltration
	Freezing point	

CHALLENGING MISCONCEPTIONS:

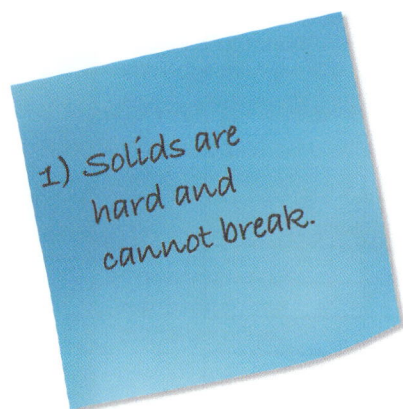

1) Solids are hard and cannot break.

2) Sand is not a solid.

3) Sunlight causes evaporation.

1+2) Children are confused by the everyday use of the word 'solid' as an adjective. Clear scientific definitions are key to challenging this misconception.

• Children to find examples of materials for each definition. Play devil's advocate by giving children jelly, a sponge and a drinking glass to sort or ask them to find something the state of which they are unsure of. Keep referring to its observable properties – Does it hold its shape? Does it take the shape of the container? Which state is it? What properties do all solids share? Are they all hard? Can they break?

• Use a USB microscope to show children sand magnified. Repeat for sugar, salt and powder. Grains and particles of powder can move past each other so can be poured and take the shape of a container, but each grain or particle is a tiny solid that keeps its shape and does not change volume.

3) Children think heat and sunlight are needed for water to evaporate.

• Observe puddles over time. Trace around the puddle outline at regular intervals, taking note of the weather conditions – Is it warm? Is it sunny?

• Set up dishes of water in a range of places including the fridge. Observe change in volume over time. In which conditions does evaporation occur? Which conditions cause water to evaporate more quickly?

QUESTIONS CHILDREN MAY ASK:

1) Which state is shaving foam?

2) Why are liquids runny?

3) Do all solids turn to liquid and all liquids turn to solid?

1) Many common items are a mix of states. Shaving foam is a mix of liquid and gas.

• Show children the measure on a can of shaving foam – how much matter is inside? Ask children to squirt foam into a measuring jug up to the volume shown. Is all the foam in the jug? Empty the can into the jug. What volume is shown? Why? Explain that foam is a mix of gas and liquid – tiny bubbles of gas are enclosed by liquid. Leave the foam to observe it over time – the bubbles will gradually pop and the gas will be released into the air, eventually leaving a puddle of sticky liquid in the bottom of the jug. What other things can children name that are a mixture of materials in different states?

2) All matter is made up of tiny, tiny particles. As a substance is heated, its particles gain more energy. It is the difference in the amount of energy of the particles that causes the different properties demonstrated by solids, liquids and gases.

• Make human models of solids, liquids and gases with children each being a particle. Particles in solids are held together very closely. This makes them very strong and difficult to break apart. Solids can also hold their own shape. The particles don't move around very much but simply vibrate in their position in the solid's structure. Children could link together closely and shake/vibrate gently. Particles in liquids are quite close to each other; however, they can move past each other very easily. This makes liquids easy to pour and is why they cannot hold their own shape, but instead take the shape of their container. Children should be linked to one or two others and move gently past each other to flow. Particles in gases move around very quickly with a lot of space between them. Gases don't just take the shape of their container, they fill the space of the container that they are in. Children should break links and continuously move all over the room in different directions.

3) Most solids and liquids can change state from one to the other but do so at different temperatures.

• Children could plan an investigation to find the melting point of different solids (avoid any solids that will burn and undergo a chemical change) and compare what happens when allowed to cool. If solids such as wax, butter and chocolate are used, this will introduce the term 'solidify'.

• Children could freeze a wide range of liquids such as olive oil, bubble bath, vinegar, etc. Do they all freeze? Do they freeze at the same temperature as water? How quickly do they melt again? (Some oils will not freeze at 0 °C - what temperature would freeze them? Are there other liquids with very low freezing points?)

• Children could research the melting points of solids such as sand, iron, gold, etc.

06 – WATER CYCLE

YEAR 4
STATES OF MATTER:
06 – WATER CYCLE

why &
how?

Look at the diagram.

**What different forms of water
can you see in the picture?**

What are clouds?

**How are they formed?
Why does it rain?**

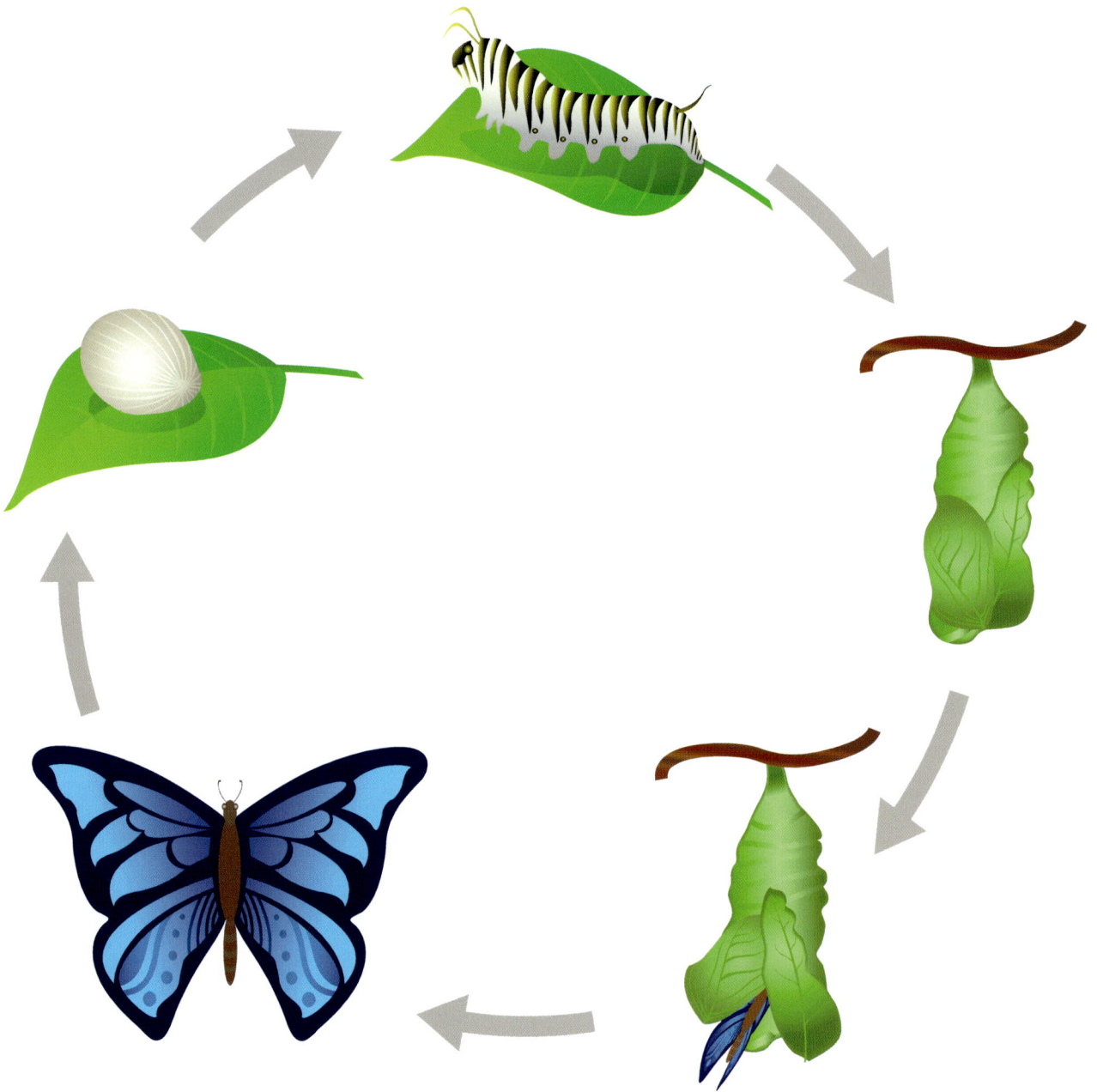

LIFE CYCLES OF PLANTS AND ANIMALS

Key concepts

- All living things (plants and animals) have a life cycle with different stages — they are born, grow, reproduce and die.

- There are differences in the life cycles of mammals, amphibians, insects and birds.

Key vocabulary:

Life cycle	Seed dispersal	Amphibian
Reproduction	Pollen	Insect
Sexual	Stamen	Bird
Asexual	Stigma	Fish
Germination	Plantlets	Reptile
Pollination	Runners	Eggs
Seed	Mammal	Live young

Activity	Resources required	Background knowledge	What to look out for
01	Flowers to pull apart. Hand lenses. Tweezers.	The key parts of a flower are petal, sepal and receptacle, then the anther and filament (stamen – male parts) and stigma, style, ovary, ovule (carpel – female parts). The only function of a flower is reproduction.	Can children name any flower parts correctly? Children may say flowers are there to attract insects – do they know why that is necessary?
02	A range of seeds from fruit, vegetables, spices, grasses, flowers and trees, e.g. conker, cumin seeds, poppy seeds, apple pips, capsicum seeds. (Whole nuts if there is no risk of an allergic reaction.)	Seeds allow a plant to make more plants similar to itself. Within each seed is an embryo – a tiny plant that will burst out of the seed case as a result of the correct combination of water, temperature and oxygen. This is called germination.	Can children name the collection as seeds? Do they understand the requirements for germination?
03	Resource sheet LIFE CYCLES OF PLANTS AND ANIMALS 3	Wind, water and animals are important to plants for pollination and seed dispersal. Flowers can be pollinated by animals, wind and water. Seeds can be dispersed by animals, wind and water. Water is also a basic requirement for plant growth. Pollination is when pollen produced by one flower is carried to another flower. Dispersal is the scattering of seeds.	Do children understand how animals, wind and water help a plant's life cycle? Do they understand the terms 'pollination' and 'dispersal'?
04	Resource sheet LIFE CYCLES OF PLANTS AND ANIMALS 4	Animals can be subdivided into reptiles, amphibians, mammals, birds, fish and invertebrates. Of these, all invertebrates, all amphibians, all birds, most reptiles and most fish lay eggs. A few reptiles and fish bear live young. Echidna and platypus are the only mammals to lay eggs – most mammals bear live young.	Do children remember the classes of animals? Are they aware of all the different classes that are egg-layers?
05	Resource sheet LIFE CYCLES OF PLANTS AND ANIMALS 5	Humans and other animals may look very different and behave very differently. But they all have one thing in common. All animals including humans are born, they get older and bigger and most will go on to have children of their own. And these children will get older and bigger and may also have children, and so on. This is called a life cycle.	Can children separate the life cycles and sequence them correctly? Can children see that all have things in common despite obvious differences?
06	Play doh	Butterflies undergo complete metamorphosis. There are four stages to the butterfly's life cycle – egg, larva (caterpillar), pupa (chrysalis) and adult.	Do children remember all the different stages of a butterfly's life cycle and how the insect changes?

LESSON ACTIVITY CARDS:

YEAR 5
LIFE CYCLES OF PLANTS AND ANIMALS
01 – PLANTS

Separate the different
parts of this flower.

Can you name any
of the parts?

What is the main function
of a flower?

YEAR 5
LIFE CYCLES OF PLANTS AND ANIMALS
02 – SEEDS

Investigate these items.
What is the name of this group of items?

How would you bring them to life?

Do all plants begin their life in the same way?
Can you think of different ways in which
a plant's life could start?

YEAR 5
LIFE CYCLES OF PLANTS AND ANIMALS
03 – PLANT LIFE CYCLE

Look at the cards.
Can you name each one?

Which ones might be
important to plants? Why?

What do the words 'pollinate'
and 'disperse' mean?

YEAR 5
LIFE CYCLES OF PLANTS AND ANIMALS
04 – EGGS

Look at the cards.
Can you sort them into reptiles, birds,
fish, amphibians, minibeasts and other?

Which groups lay eggs?

What is the name of the 'other' group?
Why don't they lay eggs?

YEAR 5
LIFE CYCLES OF PLANTS AND ANIMALS
05 – LIFE CYCLES

Examine the cards.
Can you sort them into the
different life cycles?

Can you put each life cycle
into the correct order?

What is the same about each life cycle?
What is different?

YEAR 5
LIFE CYCLES OF PLANTS AND ANIMALS
06 – BUTTERFLY

Use the play doh to recreate each
part of a butterfly's lifecycle.

Can you name each stage?

How does the insect change each time?

Download a pdf of these activity cards from our website:
pstt.org.uk/eee-resources

CHALLENGING MISCONCEPTIONS:

1) All new plants begin life as a seed.

2) The egg is the first stage of the life cycle.

3) Only birds lay eggs.

1) New plants can be created in a range of ways including planting seeds and bulbs, planting plantlets, using stolons (runners) and taking cuttings.

- Grow strawberry plants or ground ivy to see new roots forming along the stolons/runners.

- Grow from bulbs and seeds. Cut both open to explore the similarities and differences.

- Grow new veg from carrot tops, the root end of spring onions, celery bases, basil and mint stems and many more.

- Plant and grow spider plant plantlets.

2) The stages in a life cycle are repeated and there is no first or last stage.

- Discuss 'What came first, the chicken or the egg'?

- Make sure life cycles are created as a cycle/circle, not a linear path.

3) Most children understand that they came from their mother and apply the mammal style of reproduction to other living things.

- Research the life cycle of a wide range of animals including an amphibian, a reptile, a bird, a fish, an invertebrate and a mammal.

- Observe the life cycle of a stick insect or giant African Land Snail, both commonly available pet invertebrates.

- ZSL zoos run education sessions and activities on life cycles and have breeding rooms where reptile and bird eggs are hatched.

- Hatch butterflies – there are numerous kits for sale in the UK.

QUESTIONS CHILDREN MAY ASK:

1) How much of what we eat is seeds?

2) How does an egg turn into a living thing?

3) I would like to know about the life cycle of...

1) Children may be astounded by the amount of seeds we eat – either intentionally or unintentionally. Seeds are a good source of protein fibre, minerals and fat.

- Explore a selection of foods, e.g. sweetcorn, pumpkin seeds, sunflower seeds, nuts ('be aware of allergies), sugar snap peas, peas, seeded bread, cucumbers, courgettes, tomatoes, strawberries, blackberries, kiwis, bananas, passion fruit, green beans. Which of these do the children eat? Can children find the seeds in each? Which foods do we eat where we remove the seeds? Why do we remove them?

2) Eggs are comprised of shell, membrane, yolk and albumen, all of which protect and nourish the growing animal.

- Research the parts of a hen's egg and what the role of each is in the development of a chicken.

- Test each part for fat, protein, carbohydrate. The yolk contains fat, vitamins, minerals and protein and is the main source of nourishment for the growing embryo. Whereas the albumen is purely protein and initially protects the yolk.

- Hatch some chicks, candling the eggs at the appropriate times and comparing to embryo growth chart.

3) Children will have their own interests as far as animal life cycles are concerned.

- Allow children to choose an animal's life cycle to research and present in some way – models, drama, multimedia, etc.

03 – PLANT LIFE CYCLE

YEAR 5
LIFE CYCLES OF PLANTS AND ANIMALS:
03 – PLANT LIFE CYCLE

why &
how?

Look at the cards.

Can you name each one?

**Which ones might be
important to plants? Why?**

**What do the words 'pollinate'
and 'disperse' mean?**

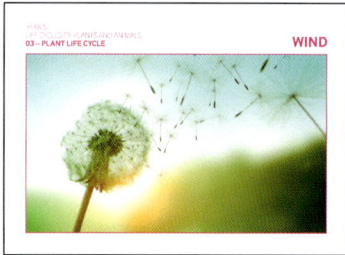

YEAR 5
LIFE CYCLES OF PLANTS AND ANIMALS
03 – PLANT LIFE CYCLE

WIND

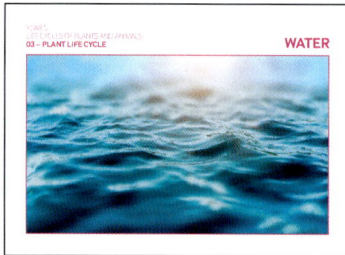

YEAR 5
LIFE CYCLES OF PLANTS AND ANIMALS
03 – PLANT LIFE CYCLE

WATER

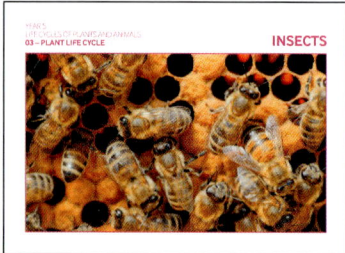

YEAR 5
LIFE CYCLES OF PLANTS AND ANIMALS
03 – PLANT LIFE CYCLE

INSECTS

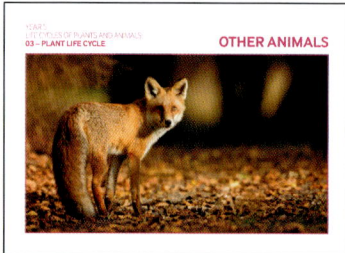

YEAR 5
LIFE CYCLES OF PLANTS AND ANIMALS
03 – PLANT LIFE CYCLE

OTHER ANIMALS

04 – EGGS

YEAR 5
LIFE CYCLES OF PLANTS AND ANIMALS:
04 – EGGS

why & how?

Look at the cards.

Can you sort them into reptiles, birds, fish, amphibians, minibeasts and other?

Which groups lay eggs?

What is the name of the 'other' group?
Why don't they lay eggs?

ZEBRA

PELICAN

SPIDER

CROCODILE

SALMON

NEWT

GOLDFISH

FROG

PARROT

LADYBIRD

COW

SEAL

PENGUIN

PIG

05 – LIFE CYCLES

YEAR 5
LIFE CYCLES OF PLANTS AND ANIMALS:
05 – LIFE CYCLES

Examine the cards.

Can you sort them into the different life cycles?

Can you put each life cycle into the correct order?

What is the same about each life cycle? What is different?

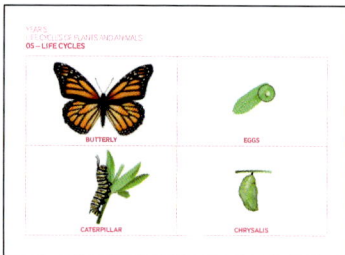

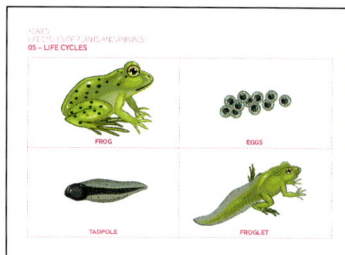

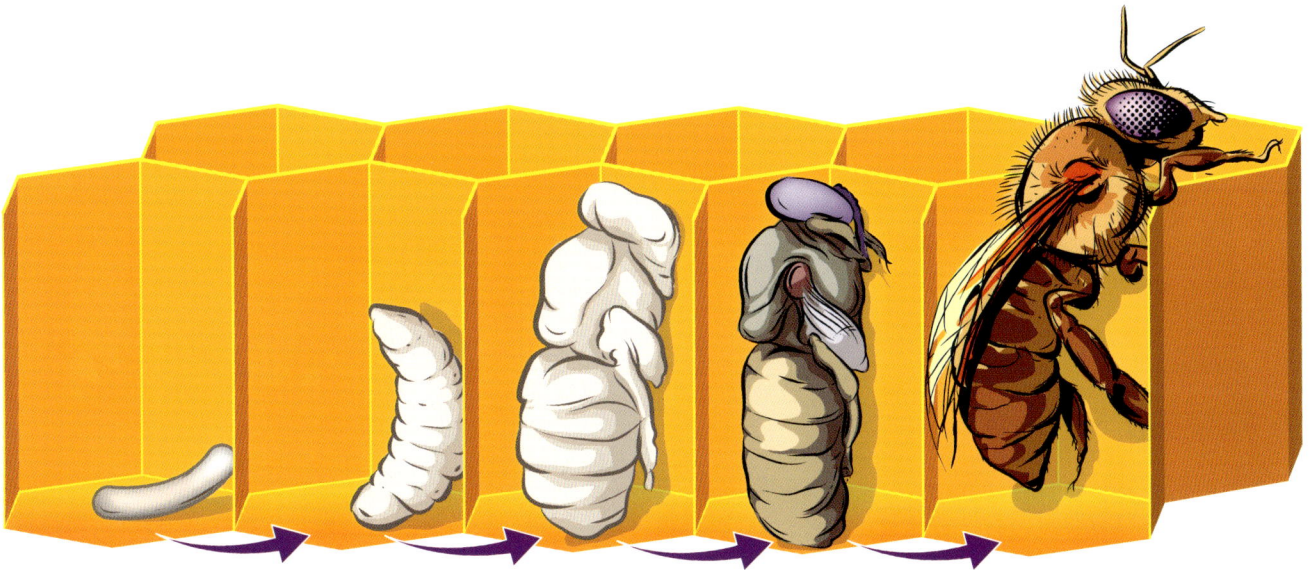

LESSON ACTIVITY CARDS:

YEAR 5
GROWTH AND DEVELOPMENT OF HUMANS
01 – TIMELINE

Examine the cards.

Can you put the cards in chronological order?

Can you name each stage?

How could we adapt this sequence to show the human life cycle?

YEAR 5
GROWTH AND DEVELOPMENT OF HUMANS
02 – HUMAN GESTATION

Examine the cards.

Can you put these cards in order of development?

How long does a human baby take to develop before it is born?

Where does a human baby develop?

YEAR 5
GROWTH AND DEVELOPMENT OF HUMANS
03 – ANIMAL GESTATION

Examine the cards.

Can you name each animal?

Order the animals according to how long their babies take to develop before being born.

Why do some take longer to develop than others?

YEAR 5
GROWTH AND DEVELOPMENT OF HUMANS
04 – BABY GROWTH

Examine the cards.

Can you put the cards into chronological order?

How much does an average newborn baby weigh?
How much does an average one year-old weigh?

Can you match the development milestones to the correct picture?

YEAR 5
GROWTH AND DEVELOPMENT OF HUMANS
05 – PUBERTY

Examine the cards.

What is puberty?

Which of these changes are linked to puberty?

Can you sort them into those affecting boys, those affecting girls and those affecting both?
Why do boys and girls experience different things?

YEAR 5
GROWTH AND DEVELOPMENT OF HUMANS
06 – HEALTH DURING PUBERTY

Examine the statements.

Which of these are necessary in order to keep healthy during puberty?

Why are each important?

Do these statements differ for boys and girls?

Download a pdf of these activity cards from our website:
pstt.org.uk/eee-resources

CHALLENGING MISCONCEPTIONS:

1) Babies develop in the stomach.

2) The 'rope' of the baby develops last.

3) The six stages of a human can be placed in a circle to create a human life cycle.

1) Children may think babies develop in the stomach.

• Use diagrams of the reproductive system to illustrate the difference between the location and size of the stomach and the womb/uterus. Discuss the different functions of each. Show how the size and location of both change as a foetus develops.

2) Children can be unaware of the name and function of the umbilical cord.

• Show children how the umbilical cord is present from the seventh week of pregnancy. Discuss what children think its role is – why does the foetus need to be attached to the mother's womb? It transports all the nutrients, oxygen and water the foetus needs in order to survive and grow.

3) In general, elderly people do not have babies.

• Discuss at what age people usually have babies. Ask children to try and represent this using the cards – which part should link to the baby? Where should the elderly person go?

QUESTIONS CHILDREN MAY ASK:

1) Why do some animals have longer gestation periods?

2) What age do you normally start puberty?

3) Why do we have pubic hair?

1) Generally, there are two main factors that contribute to the length of the gestation period for an animal. Larger animals tend to have longer gestation periods as they tend to produce larger offspring. More developed babies typically require a longer gestation period.

- Children could discover this for themselves by researching and plotting graphs to show size of offspring v gestation period, size of brain v gestation period, life span v gestation period, etc. Is there a correlation? Are there any exceptions? Why?

2) Puberty is triggered by the release of gonadotropin – releasing hormone (GnRH) from a part of the brain called the hypothalamus. This stimulates the release of other hormones and switches on the development from child to adult. The onset of puberty varies, but the average age for girls to begin puberty is 11, while for boys the average age is 12. However there's no set timetable. It's completely normal for puberty to begin at any point from the ages of 8 to 14. The process takes about four years overall.

3) There are no definitive answers as to why we have pubic hair and this is a nice current example to illustrate that we do not know everything – we are still discovering. The current theories are that pubic hair protects against friction/rubbing, traps dirt and prevents bacterial infections or that it traps pheromones secreted by apocrine glands in the groin and armpits, which will help attract a mate.

NB: It is advisable to give children the opportunity to ask questions about this topic confidentially and anonymously, e.g. posting questions in a box over the course of a few days.

01 – TIMELINE

YEAR 5
GROWTH AND DEVELOPMENT OF HUMANS:
01 – TIMELINE

Examine the cards.

Can you put the cards in chronological order?

Can you name each stage?

How could we adapt this sequence to show the human life cycle?

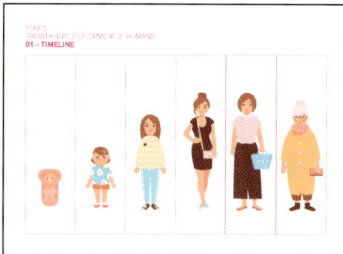

02 – HUMAN GESTATION

YEAR 5
GROWTH AND DEVELOPMENT OF HUMANS:
02 – HUMAN GESTATION

why &
how?

Examine the cards.

Can you put these cards in order of development?

How long does a human baby take to develop before it is born?

Where does a human baby develop?

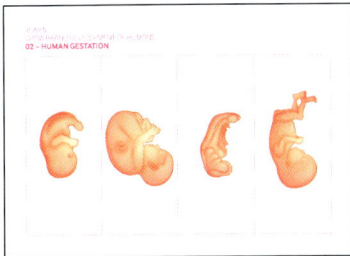

03 – ANIMAL GESTATION

YEAR 5
GROWTH AND DEVELOPMENT OF HUMANS:
03 – ANIMAL GESTATION

why & how?

Examine the cards.

Can you name each animal?

Order the animals according to how long their babies take to develop before being born.

Why do some take longer to develop than others?

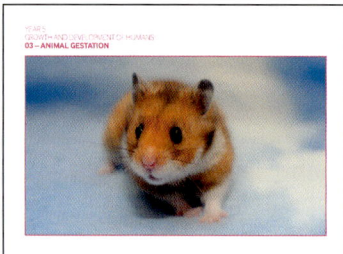

04 – BABY GROWTH

YEAR 5
GROWTH AND DEVELOPMENT OF HUMANS:
04 – BABY GROWTH

Examine the cards.

Can you put the cards into chronological order?

**How much does an average newborn baby weigh?
How much does an average one year-old weigh?**

Can you match the development milestones to the correct picture?

FOCUSSING AND SMILING	STANDING AND TAKING STEPS WITH SUPPORT	LIFTING HEAD AND SHOULDERS	WALKING
SITTING	MAKING SOUNDS	CRAWLING	FIRST WORDS

05 – PUBERTY

why&
how?

Examine the cards.

What is puberty?

**Which of these changes
are linked to puberty?**

**Can you sort them into those affecting boys,
those affecting girls and those affecting both?
Why do boys and girls experience different things?**

YEAR 5
GROWTH AND DEVELOPMENT OF HUMANS:
05 – PUBERTY

HAIR GROWTH IN ARMPITS	EYES CHANGE COLOUR	PUBIC HAIR GROWS	SKIN BECOMES OILY
TESTICLES AND PENIS GROW	BODY SWEATS MORE	FRECKLES INCREASE	GROW TALLER AND HEAVIER
MOOD SWINGS	VOICE BECOMES DEEPER	BODY CHANGES SHAPE	PERIODS BEGIN
HAIR FALLS OUT	BREASTS DEVELOP	FACIAL HAIR APPEARS	SKIN CHANGES COLOUR

06 – HEALTH DURING PUBERTY

YEAR 5
GROWTH AND DEVELOPMENT OF HUMANS:
06 – HEALTH DURING PUBERTY

why &
how?

Examine the statements.

**Which of these are necessary
in order to keep healthy during puberty?**

Why are each important?

Do these statements differ for boys and girls?

YEAR 5
GROWTH AND DEVELOPMENT OF HUMANS:
06 – HEALTH DURING PUBERTY

A HEALTHY DIET	A GIRLFRIEND OR BOYFRIEND	STRESS MANAGEMENT TECHNIQUES	LOTS OF FRIENDS
GOOD PERSONAL HYGIENE	GOOD RELATIONS WITH PARENTS	TIME OFF SCHOOL	ADEQUATE SLEEP
REGULAR EXERCISE	A HEALTHY BODY WEIGHT	GOOD ORGANISATION	SOMEONE TO TALK TO

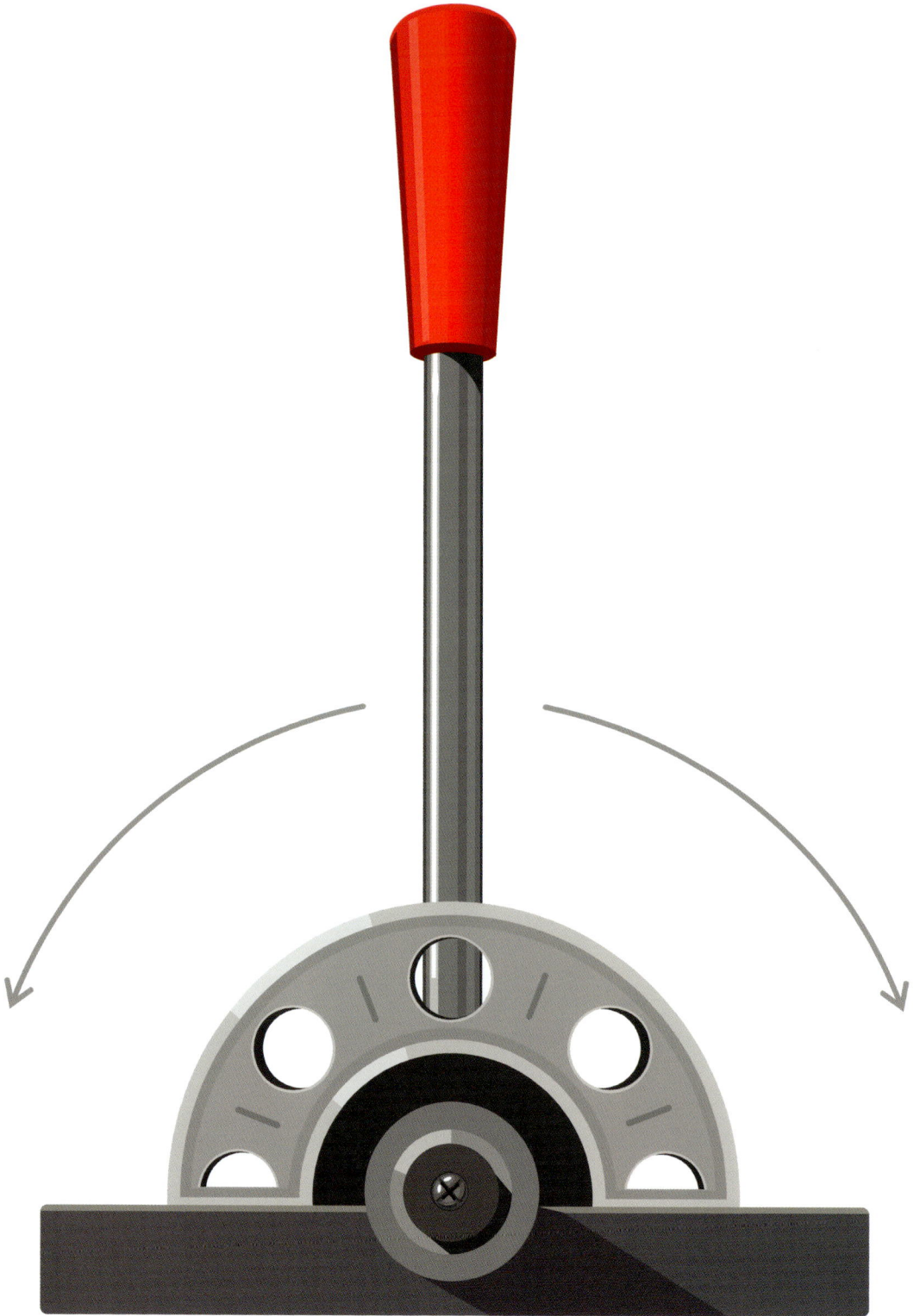

FORCES

Key concepts

- Unsupported objects fall towards the Earth because of the force of gravity acting between the Earth and the falling object.

- Air resistance, water resistance and friction act between moving surfaces.

- Air resistance, water resistance and friction slow moving objects.

- Some mechanisms, including levers, pulleys and gears, allow a smaller force to have a greater effect.

Key vocabulary:

Earth	Air resistance	Mechanism
Gravity	Water resistance	Lever
Mass	Upthrust	Pulley
Weight	Friction	Gear
Force	Moving surface	Force meter
Newton		

Activity	Resources required	Background knowledge	What to look out for
01	A large space and a foam javelin.	Forces are pushes or pulls. Javelins are propelled forwards by the push of the thrower's arm. As the javelin travels forwards through the air, air resistance is pushing back against it and gravity is pulling the javelin down. Gravity pulls the javelin to Earth even when it is on the ground.	Children may think the javelin falls because it runs out of 'push'. Do they recognise that other forces are acting? Are children using the words 'gravity' and 'air resistance'?
02	A range of shoes with different soles.	Friction is a force between two surfaces sliding across each other. Friction works in the opposite direction to which the object is moving, slowing the moving object down. The amount of friction depends on the surface of the objects. The rougher the surface, the more friction is produced.	Do children know how to use a force meter? Do children use the word 'friction'? Are they aware of its effects? Children may think that only rough surfaces cause friction.
03	A small sheet or piece of fabric – at least 1 m x 1 m in size.	Air resistance is a type of friction between air and another material. Air resistance acts against objects moving through air, including objects falling due to gravity – this is how parachutes work.	Can children explain what makes the sheet bulge? Do they use the words 'air resistance' or do they talk of trapped air?
04	A bowl of water, a range of items – some buoyant, some not. (Take care not to create misconceptions, e.g. that all metal items provided sink)	When an object is put into a liquid, two forces act on it. One is gravity, which pulls the object down, and the other is upthrust, which pushes the object up. The object pushes some of the water out of the way and it is this displaced water that causes upthrust. The size of the upthrust on the object will be equal to the weight of the water that has been displaced. If the downward pull of gravity is greater than the upthrust, the object will sink. If gravity and upthrust are equal, the object will float. The density of a material is how much there is of it (mass) in a particular volume of it. Lead has a high density, i.e. it is heavy for its size, whereas wood has a lower density, i.e. it is lighter for its size. When a material has a density greater than that of water, it will sink. If a material is less dense than water, it will float.	Children may confuse weight with density and say things such as 'it sinks because it is heavy'. Do they draw on any existing knowledge, e.g. that trees or branches, which, although they feel heavy, will float?
05	A bowl of water and a plastic plate. Resource sheet FORCES 5	When objects move in water, there is friction between them and the water. This is called water resistance. Water resistance slows down objects moving in water. Some shapes, known as streamlined shapes, cause less resistance than others. Penguins and fish are streamlined, so that they move through water as easily as possible.	Do children use the words 'friction' or 'water resistance'? Are they aware of its effects?
06	A pencil, a ruler and a weight secured to one end of the ruler.	Levers are one of the oldest and simplest machines. They consist of two parts – a beam (ruler) and a fulcrum/pivot (pencil) and allow humans to lift heavy objects by applying a small force. Levers can be classified according to the relative position of the load, fulcrum and force. In 1st Class levers, the pivot is in between the effort and the load, e.g. seesaw. In 2nd Class levers, the load is between the fulcrum and the effort, e.g. wheelbarrow. And in 3rd Class levers, the effort is between the fulcrum and the load, e.g. fishing rod.	Can children name examples of real life levers?

LESSON ACTIVITY CARDS:

**YEAR 5
FORCES:
01 – JAVELIN**

Throw the javelin as far as you can.

What makes it move forwards?

What makes it fall?

**Can you name all the forces acting on the javelin as it travels through the air?
What about when it is back on the ground?**

**YEAR 5
FORCES:
02 – SHOES**

Examine the shoes and pull each one along the floor using a force meter.

What differences can you see?

Can you feel any differences as you pull them?

Why do you think this is?

**YEAR 5
FORCES:
03 – SHEET**

Take a corner of the sheet each.

**What happens when you lift it up together?
What happens if you pull it down together?**

Why does this happen?

Can you think of uses of this in real life?

**YEAR 5
FORCES:
04 – FLOATING AND SINKING**

Place each item in the water, one at a time.

Which ones float and which ones sink?

Why do some float and some sink?

**Can you name something else that would float?
Can you name something else that would sink?**

**YEAR 5
FORCES:
05 – PLATE**

Push the plate along in the water as shown in the diagram.

What differences do you notice?

Why are there differences?

How do fish and boats take advantage of this?

**YEAR 5
FORCES:
06 – LEVERS**

Lift the weight by pushing on the opposite end of the ruler. Repeat, moving the pencil to different positions along the ruler.

When is the weight easier to lift?

Why do you think this is?

Can you think of examples of levers used in everyday life?

Download a pdf of these activity cards from our website:
pstt.org.uk/eee-resources

CHALLENGING MISCONCEPTIONS:

1) Heavy objects sink, light objects float.

2) Heavy objects fall faster.

3) Friction occurs between two solids.

1) If the weight of an object is equal to or less than the upthrust pushing against it, the object will float. A heavy object can be made to float if its shape means that it displaces a greater volume of water than its weight, e.g. a ship.

• Show children images of container ships.

• Investigate a range of different items – weigh them with a force meter and then test to see if they float or sink. Can children find a light object that sinks? Can children find a heavy object that floats?

• Demonstrate a ball of plasticine sinking. Can children make it float by changing its shape? Create a class challenge – in small groups. give each group the same amount of plasticine and challenge them to make it float AND hold marbles – who can hold the greatest number of marbles? The weight of the object (plasticine) will be the same for each group, but they can change its shape to increase the amount of upthrust so that it will float.

2) Heavy and light objects fall at the same rate. Air resistance slows down the fall of objects. Objects with a greater surface area will cause greater air resistance.

• Use two identical plastic bottles – one empty and one filled with water. Pass round so that children can feel the difference in weight. Ask children to predict which one would fall faster, giving reasons for their predictions. Drop both bottles from the same height. at the same time – as high as is safely possible. Which one hits the ground first? Why? (Film in slow motion to help with observations.)

• Use two sheets of A4 paper – one flat and one screwed into a ball. Ask children to predict which one would fall faster. giving reasons for their predictions. Drop both pieces of paper from the same height, at the same time – as high as is safely possible. Which one hits the ground first? Why?

• Set a question for children to investigate – how can you make an egg fall slower? Give all children an egg of similar size and weight to adapt and make fall slower. Test by dropping – if the height is great enough drop one by one and time; if the height isn't great enough. drop all at the same time and see which hits the floor last. (Film in slow motion to help with observations.)

3) Friction occurs between all surfaces and materials, including air and water. Friction produced between water and a moving object is called water resistance. Friction produced between air and a moving object is called air resistance.

• Demonstrate air resistance by asking children to run across the playground holding a large sheet of card in front of them. What do they feel? This is air pushing against the movement and is a type of friction.

• Investigate air resistance by modifying sportswear to create maximum air resistance.

• Demonstrate water resistance by repeating activity Forces 5. Which way round did the children feel the biggest push against the plate?

• Investigate how animals use increased/ decreased water and air resistance to help them. e.g. flippers and webbed feet. streamlined shapes. wings. etc.

QUESTIONS CHILDREN MAY ASK:

1) Why do some things float then sink?

2) Why do parachutes fail sometimes?

3) How do planes stay in the air?

1) Porous objects have many small holes, so liquid or air can pass through. These objects may initially float as the holes full of air make the object more buoyant. However, when these holes fill with water, the weight of the object increases and the object may sink.

- Children could use a microscope to compare the porosity of objects and materials and look for a link between porosity and floating/sinking.

2) The large surface area of an open parachute creates a lot of air resistance, which pushes against the pull of gravity and slows down the descent. Parachutes can fail to open for a variety of reasons, e.g. the release mechanism does not work, the parachute gets tangled. Whenever a parachute only opens partially or does not open at all, the surface area will be decreased and will not be great enough to slow down the descent effectively.

- Arrange a visitor to show children a parachute – how it is packed, how it is released, how it opens and the procedures to follow if it fails.

3) There are four forces acting on a plane as it takes off and flies – thrust from the engine, which pushes the plane forwards, air resistance or drag, which works against the forward movement, gravity, which pulls the plane to Earth and lift, which holds the plane in the air. Daniel Bernoulli discovered that the faster air flows over the surface of something, the less the air pushes on that surface (and so the lower its pressure). The wings of a plane are aerofoils, which means they are shaped to make air flow faster over the top, causing higher pressure beneath the wings and creating lift.

- Demonstrate the Bernoulli principle. Turn on a hair dryer to the highest setting and point it straight up. Ask children to predict what will happen if you place a ping pong ball in the air flow and ask them to give reasons for their predictions. Carefully place a ping pong ball in the stream of air. Why doesn't the ping pong ball fly into the air?

- Observe and sketch birds' and planes' wings. What do children notice about the shape?

- Demonstrate how an aerofoil creates lift by making a paper aerofoil. Make a line across a piece of paper to form two unequal parts. Make a light fold along the line – do not crease heavily. Bring the corners of the paper together causing the longer side to arch and secure with tape. With a sharp pencil carefully make a hole through the top and bottom of the wing near the front edge. Push a straw through, – this may need to be glued into place if it does not fit snugly enough. Cut a long piece of string and thread it through the straw, making sure that it doesn't catch and can move easily up and down it. Hold the string tight and blow air from a hair dryer or fan towards the curved edge. It will move up the string.

05 – PLATE

why&
how?

Push the plate along in the water as shown in the diagram.

What differences do you notice?

Why are there differences?

How do fish and boats take advantage of this?

05 – PLATE

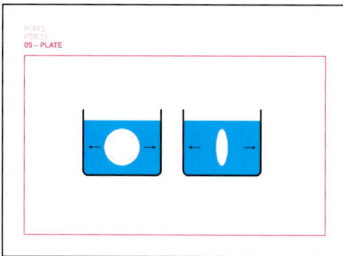

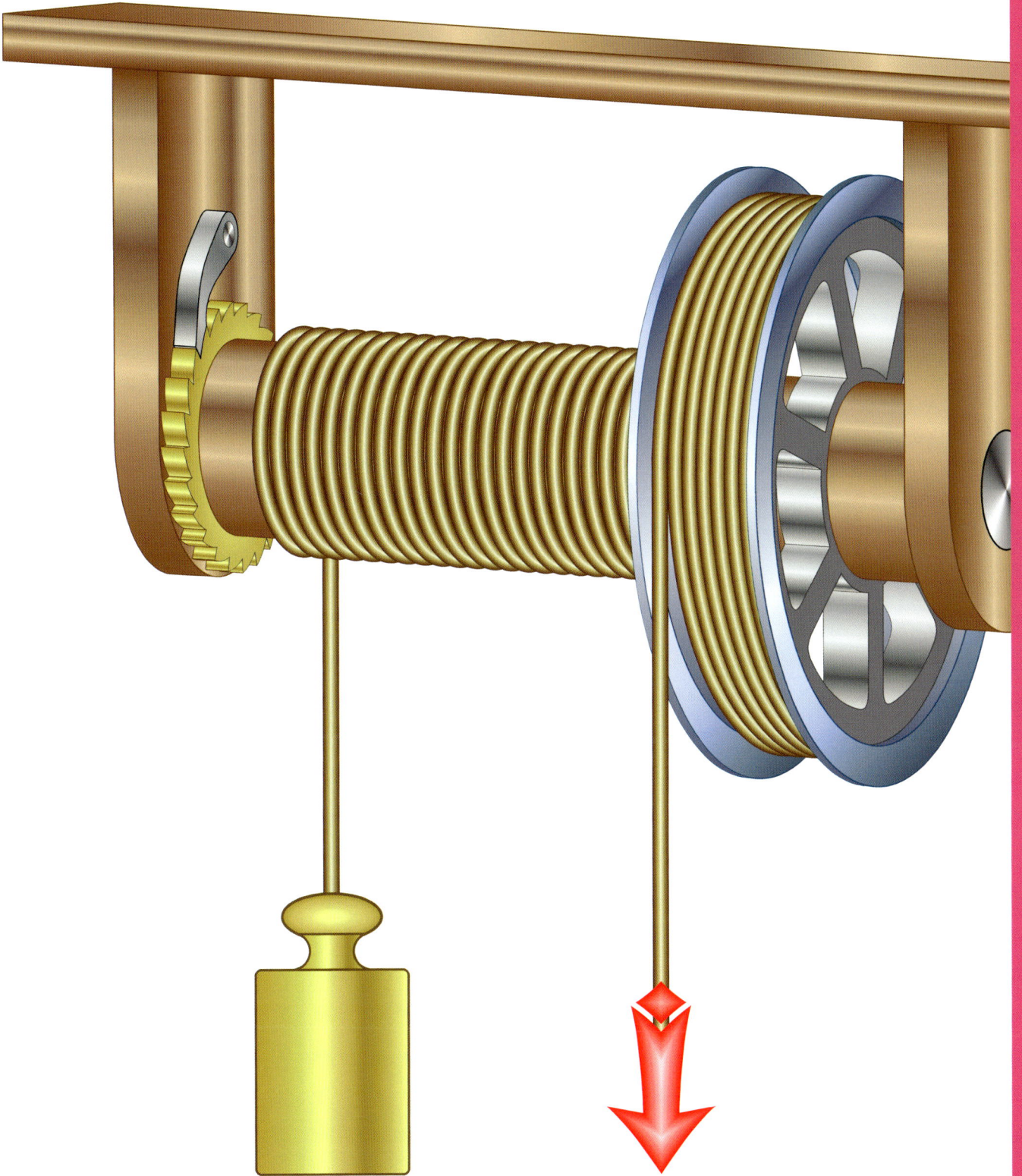

EARTH AND SPACE

Key concepts

- The Sun, Earth and Moon are approximately spherical bodies.

- The Sun is a star at the centre of our solar system.

- The Earth and other planets orbit the Sun.

- A Moon is a celestial body that orbits a planet.

- Earth has one Moon and the Moon's orbit gives rise to the phases of the Moon we observe on earth.

- The Earth's rotation about its axis explains day and night and the apparent movement of the Sun across the sky.

Key vocabulary:

Earth	Rotate	Uranus
Planet	Rotation	Neptune
Sun	Night and day	Pluto
Solar system	Mercury	'Dwarf' planet
Moon	Venus	Orbit
Celestial body	Mars	Revolve
Sphere	Jupiter	
Spherical	Saturn	

Activity	Resources required	Background knowledge	What to look out for
01	A range of spherical objects of different sizes, but including a peppercorn and an inflatable beach ball.	If the Earth was the size of a pea, the Moon would be the size of a peppercorn and the Sun would be the size of a beach ball. If the Earth was the size of a pea, then the Moon would be about 25 cm away from the Earth and the Sun would be about 100 m away.	Are children aware that the Moon only appears as big as the Sun due to its proximity to Earth?
02	Resource sheet EARTH AND SPACE 2	Stars are spheres of superhot gas generally made up of helium and hydrogen. Planets are large spherical objects that orbit a star. In our solar system we have eight planets – Mercury, Venus, Earth, Mars, Jupiter, Saturn, Uranus and Neptune. Pluto was reclassified as a dwarf planet in 2006. Moons are natural objects that orbit planets. Other natural objects in space include comets, asteroids, meteors and meteorites.	Are children aware of the differences between stars, planets and Moons? Do children know that our Sun is a star?
03	Resource sheet EARTH AND SPACE 3	The planets are all roughly spherical. Mercury, Venus, Earth and Mars are solid and rocky whereas Jupiter, Saturn and Neptune are giant gas planets. The planets listed in order of their distance from the Sun are: Mercury, Venus, Earth, Mars, Jupiter, Saturn, Uranus and Neptune. Because of their differing size, composition and distance from the Sun, the planets experience very different atmospheres, surface gravity and temperatures.	Can children appreciate the effect that a planet's distance from the Sun has on the average temperature experienced?
04	A selection of spherical objects.	The Earth orbits the Sun and this takes 365.25 days, or one year. The Earth also rotates on its axis once every 24 hours – this causes day and night on Earth – day is experienced when parts of the Earth face the Sun and night is experienced when they are facing away from the Sun.	Children may think the Sun moves around the Earth. They may not know that the Earth orbits the Sun whilst rotating on its own axis.
05	A selection of spherical objects.	The Moon orbits the Earth every 27 days and, during this time, it rotates on its axis just once. This means that, from Earth, we always see the same side of the Moon, so never see the other side (the 'dark side'). We only see the part of the Moon that is illuminated by the Sun – the amount of the Moon that is illuminated changes as the Moon orbits the Earth.	Do the children know that the Moon orbits Earth? Children may think the Earth's shadow falling on the Moon causes the differing shapes we see.
06	Resource sheet EARTH AND SPACE 6	The Sun appears to move across the sky as each day progresses. This is actually because the Earth is rotating on its axis once every 24 hours.	Do children think the Sun moves around the Earth or do they know that the Sun appears to move because the Earth is rotating on its own axis?

LESSON ACTIVITY CARDS:

Card 01

YEAR 5
EARTH AND SPACE:
01 – SIZE

why & how?

Which is biggest...the Earth, the Sun or the Moon?
Which is the smallest?

Look at the different objects.

If the Earth was the size of a pea, which of these
would represent the Sun? What about the Moon?

If the Earth was the size of a pea, how far away
from Earth would the Moon and Sun be?

Card 02

YEAR 5
EARTH AND SPACE:
02 – CELESTIAL BODIES

why & how?

Look at the pictures.

Can you sort them using the headings?

What other natural objects
can be found in space?

Can you explain the difference between
a star, a planet and a Moon?

Card 03

YEAR 5
EARTH AND SPACE:
03 – PLANETS OF OUR SOLAR SYSTEM

why & how?

Look at the planets.

What is the same about them?
What is different?

Can you order them from closest
to the Sun to furthest away?

Why do you think there are
differences in the planets?

Card 04

YEAR 5
EARTH AND SPACE:
04 – ORBITS, THE SUN AND EARTH

why & how?

Choose two objects to represent the Sun and Earth.

Which of these move in
the solar system?

Use the models to show
the movement.

Why do we have day and night?

Card 05

YEAR 5
EARTH AND SPACE:
05 – ORBITS, EARTH AND THE MOON

why & how?

Choose two objects to represent the Moon and Earth.

Which of these move in
the solar system?

Use the models to show
the movement.

Why does the Moon appear
as different shapes?

Card 06

YEAR 5
EARTH AND SPACE:
06 – THE SUN IN THE SKY

why & how?

Look at the picture.

How will the position of the Sun change?

Why does this happen?

How often does this happen?

Download a pdf of these activity cards from our website:
pstt.org.uk/eee-resources

CHALLENGING MISCONCEPTIONS:

1) The Sun rotates around the Earth.

2) The Sun is a planet.

3) The Moon comes out at night.

1) Children can be confused by the fact that the Sun appears to move across the sky. Observing this can understandably lead to the assumption that the Sun is moving around Earth, when in fact the Sun's apparent movement is caused by the Earth rotating on its own axis.

• Use a swivel chair to recreate the motion of Earth and a static lamp to represent the Sun. Children sitting in the chair aren't moving, the Earth (chair) is, but the lamp seems to move across their line of vision, just like the Sun appears to move in our sky.

2) Key vocabulary and simple definitions need introducing and reinforcing.

• How could children write the word as a calligram which shows its meaning?

How might children sign the word to show its meaning? All children could draw/create their own version then share their ideas and reasons behind them. Adopt the best idea as the class calligram or sign.

Label as 'example of calligrams'.

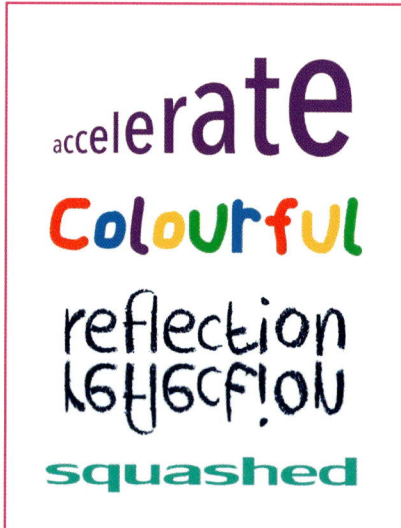

accele**rate**

Colourful

reflection
reflection

squashed

3) The Moon and stars are in the sky all the time. But you cannot usually see the stars in the day as the sunlight is so bright that it overpowers the faint light from all other stars. The Moon can be seen in the daytime sky for much of every month — excluding a few days around the new Moon. It doesn't seem as bright in the day as it does at night because the sky around it is brighter.

• Stars appear faint. So to gather enough light to resolve an image would require widening our pupils but, during the day, our eyes can't do that or they would be damaged by the bright sunlight. You can only see stars clearly after your eyes have experienced nothing but darkness for a long time. This is also why you can't see many (if any) stars when you're in a city with lots of lights, or standing underneath a street light. Show how the pupil of your eye widens and contracts by observing a partner's pupil in the light of the classroom, and then comparing how it looks straight after covering their eyes for a minute or so.

• To help spot the Moon during the day, investigate the time and direction of moonrise and moonset in your location.

QUESTIONS CHILDREN MAY ASK:

1) How big is...? How far is...?

2) How many times does the Earth spin round in a year?

3) Why does the Moon change shape?

1) Children always have lots of questions about all the different parts of our solar system. How big? How far? How cold/hot? What is ...made of?

• In pairs, research key facts about a different part of the solar system to create a class set of 'Top Trumps' cards. Children could then create a set of rules with which to play a game with these cards.

• Small groups to make a scale model of the different planets and label with key facts.

2) Children need to know the difference between rotate/spin and orbit. The Earth rotates on its axis once every twenty-four hours – this causes day and night. Earth orbits the Sun once every year (365 days, 5 hours, 48 minutes, and 46 seconds). The tilt of the Earth's axis during this orbit causes our seasons.

• Use actions to reinforce the difference between orbit and rotate.

• Use two spherical objects or one spherical object and a lamp to model the movement of the Earth around the Sun.

• Use animations to reinforce this concept.

• In groups, ask children to replicate the movement of the Earth as a human model.

3) The Moon orbits the Earth once every 27 days as the Earth is orbiting the Sun and rotating on its axis. We only see the part of the Moon that is illuminated by the Sun.

• Create a Moon phase board that children can put over their heads to better visualise the cause of the phases and the views we have.

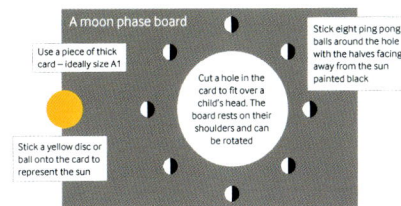

A moon phase board

Use a piece of thick card – ideally size A1

Stick a yellow disc or ball onto the card to represent the sun

Cut a hole in the card to fit over a child's head. The board rests on their shoulders and can be rotated

Stick eight ping pong balls around the hole with the halves facing away from the sun painted black

• Reinforce the names of the different phases using Oreo biscuits – remove top biscuit layer and scrape off cream to required shape and size.

• Keep a Moon diary – record the Moon's appearance over the course of a month.

02 – CELESTIAL BODIES

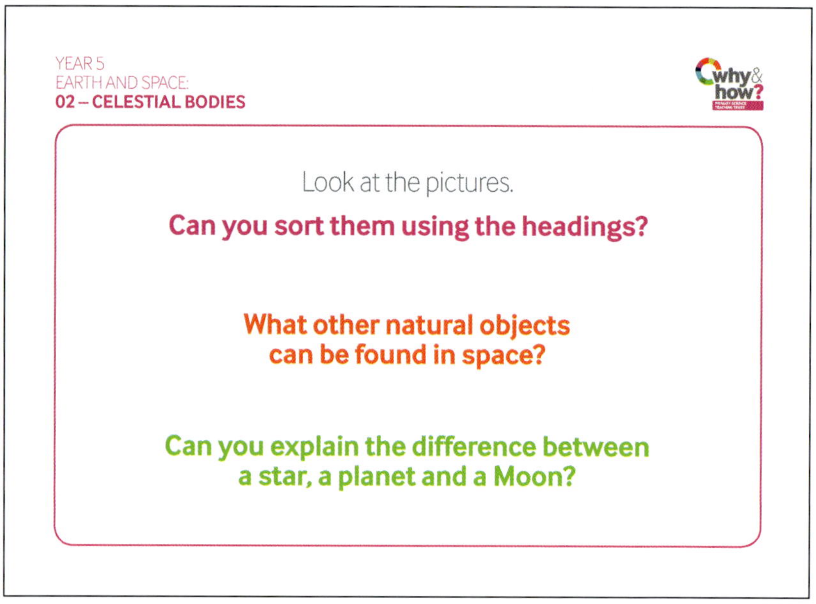

YEAR 5
EARTH AND SPACE:
02 – CELESTIAL BODIES
why & how?
Look at the pictures.
Can you sort them using the headings?
What other natural objects can be found in space?
Can you explain the difference between a star, a planet and a Moon?

02 – CELESTIAL BODIES
PLANET
STAR
MOON
NONE OF THESE

02 – CELESTIAL BODIES
THE SUN
EARTH
THE MOON
PLUTO
GANYMEDE
NEPTUNE
JUPITER
MARS

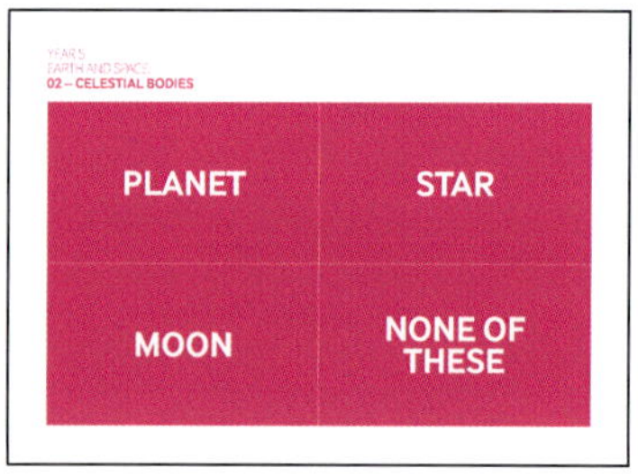

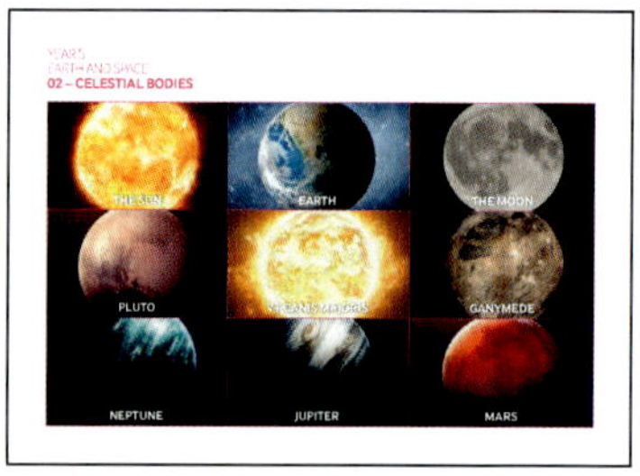

03 – PLANETS OF OUR SOLAR SYSTEM

YEAR 5
EARTH AND SPACE:
03 – PLANETS OF OUR SOLAR SYSTEM

why &
how?

Look at the planets.

**What is the same about them?
What is different?**

**Can you order them from closest
to the Sun to furthest away?**

**Why do you think there are
differences in the planets?**

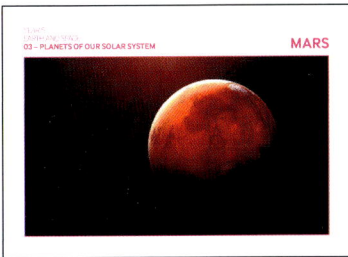

MARS

JUPITER

EARTH

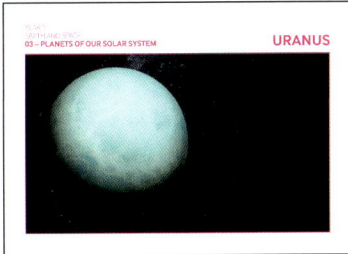

URANUS

VENUS

MERCURY

SATURN

NEPTUNE

06 – THE SUN IN THE SKY

YEAR 5
EARTH AND SPACE:
06 – THE SUN IN THE SKY

why & how?

Look at the picture.

How will the position of the Sun change?

Why does this happen?

How often does this happen?

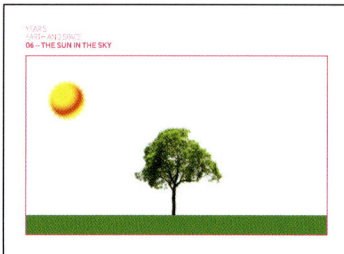

PROPERTIES AND CHANGES OF MATERIALS

Key concepts

- Everyday materials can be compared and grouped on the basis of their properties, including their hardness, solubility, transparency, conductivity (electrical and thermal), and response to magnets.

- Some solid materials will dissolve in liquid to form a solution and others will not.

- Substances can be separated from a solution.

- Mixtures can be separated through filtering, sieving and evaporating.

- The properties of materials relate to how they are used and this has changed over time.

- Dissolving, mixing and changes of state are reversible changes.

- Some changes result in the formation of new materials, and this kind of change is not usually reversible, including changes associated with burning and the action of acid on bicarbonate of soda.

Key vocabulary:

Hard	Transparent	Conductivity	Solvent
Soft	Opaque	Change state	Particle
Elastic	Translucent	Melting	Mix
Rigid	Reflective	Solid	Mixture
Flexible	Non reflective	Liquid	Filtering
Waterproof	Magnetic	Gas	Sieving
Absorbent	Attract	Dissolve	Evaporating
Strong	Solubility	Solution	Residue
Weak	Electrical	Soluble	Burn
Rough	Conductivity	Insoluble	Reversible
Smooth	Thermal	Solute	Irreversible

Activity	Resources required	Background knowledge	What to look out for
01	A range of materials – some absorbent, some magnetic, some flexible, etc.	Materials can be sorted on the basis of the following properties: Transparent materials let light through and you can see through them. Opaque materials do not let any light through and you cannot see through them. Translucent materials let some light through but you cannot easily see through them. Waterproof materials do not let water through and do not soak up water. Absorbent materials soak up water and let water pass through them. Strong materials are very difficult to break and weak materials break easily. Flexible materials are easy to bend, whereas rigid materials are difficult to bend. Hard materials are difficult to scratch. Magnetic materials are attracted to magnets. Some materials are good conductors of heat or electricity. This means that heat or electricity can travel through them easily. Some materials are insulators of heat or electricity. This means that they do not allow heat or electricity to travel through them very easily.	What vocabulary are the children using while sorting? Are they using terms such as 'rigid', 'hard', 'flexible', 'magnetic', 'insulator', 'conductor', 'opaque', 'transparent', 'translucent'?
02	Three clear, sealed, labelled containers each containing one of the following: granulated sugar, white powder paint and flour.	A reversible change is a change that can be undone or reversed. If you can get back the substances you started the reaction with, that's a reversible reaction. A reversible change might change how a material looks or feels, but it doesn't create new materials. Examples of reversible reactions include mixing, dissolving, evaporation, melting and freezing.	Do children recognise that sugar will dissolve? Do they recognise that all three solids can be separated by evaporating the water?
03	A clear, sealed, labelled container containing a mix of rice, paperclips, water, sand and mud all mixed together.	A mixture made of solid particles of different sizes, for example sand and gravel, can be separated by sieving. A mixture of water and an insoluble substance like sand can be separated by filtering. A mixture of water and a soluble substance like salt can be separated by boiling the solution. The water will evaporate until it is all gone. The salt will be left behind. If the water vapour that evaporates is collected, it can be cooled to form water again.	How many different items would they separate using their suggestions? Are they talking of sieving, filtering, evaporating?
04	Resource sheet PROPERTIES AND CHANGES OF MATERIALS 4 or real examples of each card.	Materials have different properties that make them useful for different jobs (see activity 01 in this table.) For example, metals like copper are strong, hard and shiny materials that can be hammered into different shapes without breaking and can be therefore used to make coins. Plastics are strong and waterproof and can be made into any shape by applying heat, and are therefore used to make all sorts of bottles and toys.	Are children relating function and properties using scientific vocabulary such as 'conductor', 'rigid', 'flexible', 'hard', 'transparent', etc.?
05	Two trays, each with a crayon, a piece of bread, a knob of butter, some chocolate and some pastry. Heat one tray in the oven for ten mins prior to the activity.	A change is called irreversible if it cannot be changed back again. In an irreversible change, new materials are always formed, e.g. when you mix vinegar and bicarbonate of soda the reaction produces bubbles of gas. Heating can cause an irreversible change. For example, you heat a raw egg to cook it. The cooked egg cannot be changed back to a raw egg again. Burning is an example of an irreversible change. When you burn wood, you get ash and smoke. You cannot change the ash and smoke back to wood again. Melting however is a reversible change.	Do children recognise that heat has caused changes and some are irreversible?\n\nChildren may think that the melted crayon cannot be changed back again if they focus on the original shape.
06	Bicarbonate of soda and vinegar. Small plastic cups and spoons for mixing (one set per group of children.)	Mixing substances can cause an irreversible change. For example, when vinegar and bicarbonate of soda are mixed, the mixture changes and lots of bubbles of carbon dioxide are made. These bubbles, and the liquid mixture left behind, cannot be turned back into vinegar and bicarbonate of soda again.	Do children think that the vinegar can be evaporated to leave behind the bicarbonate? What do they think the bubbles are? Many children think all gas is 'air', which they do not realise is a mixture of a range of different gases.

LESSON ACTIVITY CARDS:

YEAR 5
PROPERTIES AND CHANGES OF MATERIALS:
01 – GROUPING MATERIALS

Investigate the materials in this tray.

Can you sort any of the materials into groups?

What headings should be put on the groups?
Which words could you use to describe them?

Can you sort them another way?
How many different ways can you sort them?

YEAR 5
PROPERTIES AND CHANGES OF MATERIALS:
02 – MIXING POWDERS

Observe the sugar, paint powder and flour in the jars.

What will happen to each when mixed with water?

Can you get each solid back out of the water?

How?

YEAR 5
PROPERTIES AND CHANGES OF MATERIALS:
03 – SEPARATING MIXTURES

Look carefully at the mixture.

How could each different item be separated?

What equipment might be needed?

What would you do first? What next? Etc.

YEAR 5
PROPERTIES AND CHANGES OF MATERIALS:
04 – USES OF MATERIALS

Look at the materials and the objects.

Can you match each material to the object it would be suitable for?

What makes each material suitable for the object you have chosen?

Which material would NOT be suitable for each object and why?

YEAR 5
PROPERTIES AND CHANGES OF MATERIALS:
05 – CHANGED MATERIALS

Observe each item on the trays.

What has happened to each?

Why has this happened?

Which of these can be changed back again? How?

YEAR 5
PROPERTIES AND CHANGES OF MATERIALS:
06 – BUBBLES

Mix the powder and vinegar.

Describe what happens.

Why does this happen?

What is left in the beaker?

Download a pdf of these activity cards from our website:
pstt.org.uk/eee-resources

CHALLENGING MISCONCEPTIONS:

1) Sugar disappears when mixed with water.

2) When salt is mixed with water you cannot get it back.

3) Just the vinegar is left once it is mixed with bicarbonate of soda.

1) Sugar and other soluble solids do not disappear when mixed with water; they dissolve, which means they break down into particles that are too small to be seen. Sugar and salt can still be tasted in the solution and the mass of the solution will be equivalent to the mass of the solid and the mass of the solvent added together. This reaction is reversible.

• Use brown sugar dissolved in water so that the children can observe that the colour of a brown sugar solution is brown, demonstrating that the sugar is still there but broken down.

• Allow children to taste a sugar/salt solution to show that the solid has not disappeared – the solution tastes sweet/salty.

• Weigh the mass of the water, container and sugar/salt separately. Dissolve the sugar/salt in the water and ask children to predict the mass of the solution and container. Weigh and share result.

• Investigate the saturation point of water at different temperatures – how much sugar can be dissolved in water at room temperature, etc?

2) When solids such as salt and sugar are dissolved, this is a reversible change and the solids can be recovered by evaporating the water.

• Make two separate solutions by mixing salt with water, and sugar with water. Set up shallow, open dishes of sugar or salt solution and allow the water to evaporate overnight, leaving the sugar or salt behind in the dish. Observe.

• Investigate the dissolved solids in different waters – tap water, mineral water, flavoured water. What is left behind once the water has evaporated? Where have these come from?

3) Mixing substances can cause an irreversible change. For example, when vinegar and bicarbonate of soda are mixed, the mixture changes and lots of bubbles of carbon dioxide are made. These bubbles and the liquid mixture left behind cannot be turned back into vinegar and bicarbonate of soda again.

• Create an analogy for the difference between reversible and irreversible reactions by mixing red and yellow beads and red and yellow paints. What is the result of mixing red and yellow beads? Can you separate them again? Mixture formed and can be separated again. What is the result of mixing red and yellow paint? Can you separate them again? New colour formed and can't be separated again.

• Mix together bicarbonate of soda and vinegar by placing the powder in a balloon and the vinegar in a bottle and carefully stretching the neck of the balloon over the neck of the bottle without tipping in any powder. Ask children what is inside the balloon/bottle combo. Tip the bicarbonate of soda into the vinegar and observe/describe the reaction. What happened to the balloon? Why? Where has the extra gas come from? Can we mix it back into the liquid to get the vinegar and bicarbonate of soda back?

• Compare mixing materials that create a chemical reaction, e.g. grout/ fizzy vitamin tablet and water, and those that do not, e.g. flour/paint/salt with water. How are they the same? How are they different? Leave all mixtures open overnight and observe/ compare in the morning. How are they the same? How are they different? Which mixtures have created a new material?

• Ensure that children experience other irreversible reactions caused by burning, rusting, cooking and heating too.

QUESTIONS CHILDREN MAY ASK:

1) What is the difference between melting and dissolving?

2) What is the gas produced when vinegar and bicarbonate of soda are mixed?

3) How can a mix of flour, water and sugar be separated?

1) In order to melt something you need only one substance. When a solid melts, it changes from a solid state into a liquid state, usually due to the application of heat – no other substance is involved. In order to dissolve something there needs to be two substances – a solute (the solid) and a solvent (usually water in primary school). In the solid the particles are bonded together. When a solid dissolves, these particles become surrounded by the solvent and are no longer bonded to each other and can flow with the solvent in a mixture called a solution. Both of these reactions are reversible.

• Compare melting and dissolving by melting and dissolving a range of different solids and observing. For each solid, children should think about what happens to the solid during the process, what other substances are involved and what happens if the results are left overnight.

• Reinforce the meaning of MELT and DISSOLVE by thinking of an action that can be done to represent what happens to the solid in each case. How could we show that the solid turns to a liquid in an action? How could we show the solid breaking down into tiny particles to demonstrate dissolving?

2) Bicarbonate of soda mixed with vinegar produces carbon dioxide. Gases cause special difficulties for children since those commonly experienced, like air, are invisible. Many are not able to name individual gases.

• Demonstrate how the gas produced is not 'air'. Light a tea light candle, tip a glass of air over the flame – what happens? Nothing. Now mix a teaspoon of bicarbonate of soda with a tablespoon of distilled vinegar in another glass. Once the reaction has subsided, tip the gas over the flame, being careful not to tip any liquid out too. What happens? The flame is extinguished by the carbon dioxide. The carbon dioxide is denser than air, so it sits in the bottom of the glass. When you pour the gas from the glass onto the candle, you are pouring out the carbon dioxide, which will sink and displace the air surrounding the candle with carbon dioxide. This suffocates the flame and it goes out.

3) Sugar dissolves to form a solution when mixed with water, flour does not. Flour could be filtered out and then the sugar solution left open so that the water evaporates.

• Let children discover this by trial and error. Set a class challenge. Ask children to suggest ways in which these different materials could be separated and let them investigate in groups. Offer a range of equipment including red herrings such as microscopes, sieves, syringes.

04 – USES OF MATERIALS

YEAR 5
PROPERTIES AND CHANGES OF MATERIALS:
04 – USES OF MATERIALS

why &
how?

Look at the materials and the objects.

Can you match each material to the object it would be suitable for?

What makes each material suitable for the object you have chosen?

Which material would NOT be suitable for each object and why?

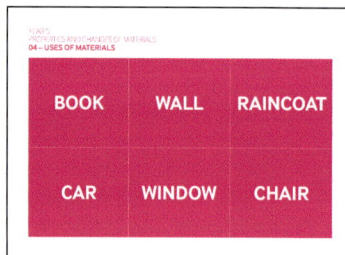

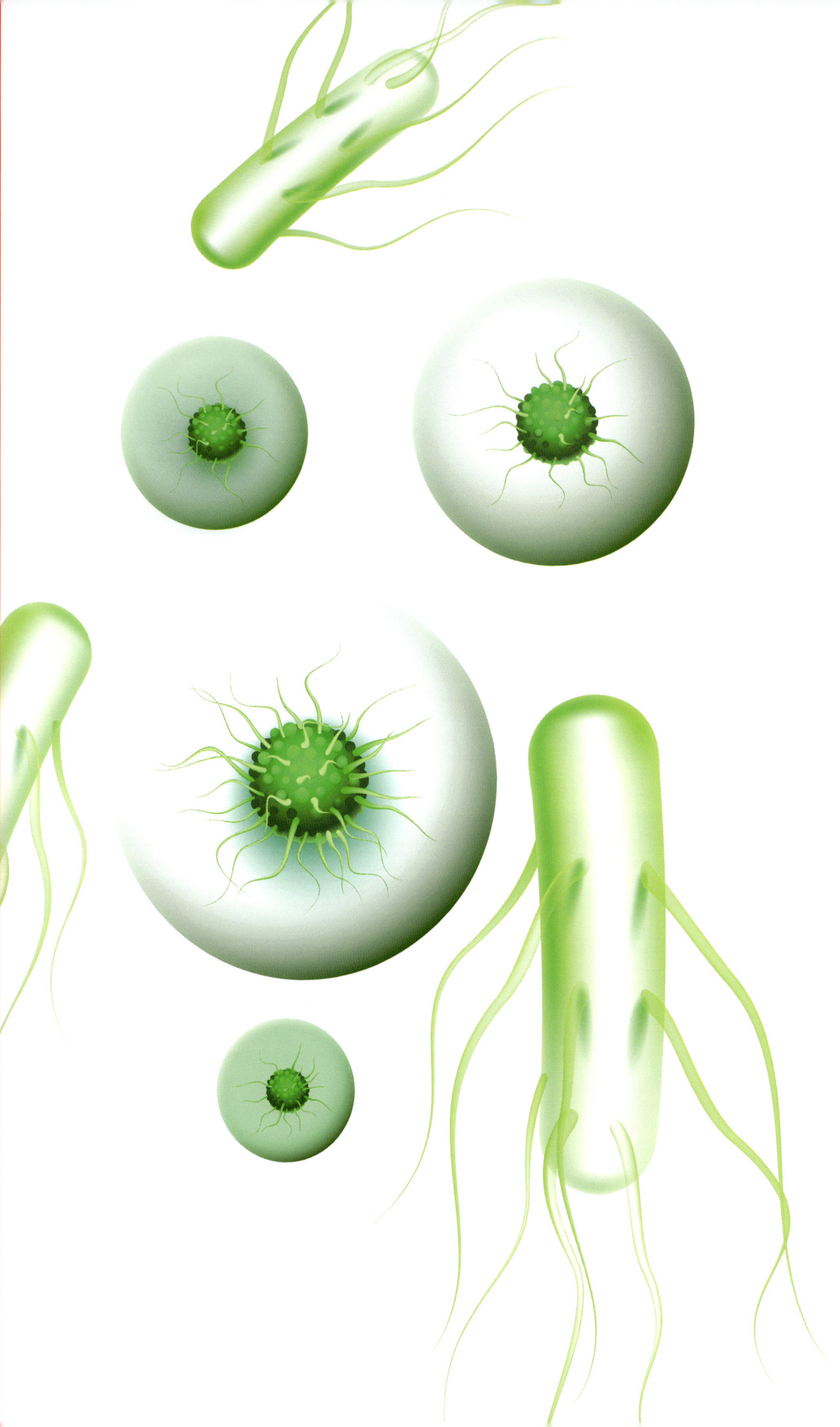

CLASSIFYING PLANTS AND ANIMALS

Key concepts

- Living things are classified into broad groups according to common observable characteristics and based on similarities and differences, including microorganisms, plants and animals.

Key vocabulary:

Organism	Fish	Vertebrate	Crustacean
Microorganism	Amphibian	Invertebrate	Classification key
Fungus	Reptile	Arachnid	Environment
Bacteria	Bird	Mollusc	
Virus	Mammal	Insect	

Activity	Resources required	Background knowledge	What to look out for
01	A selection of different leaves.	Leaf identification is one of the best ways to identify trees. There are two main types of leaf, a simple leaf made up of one leaf or a compound leaf made up of many smaller leaves. Leaves come in many different shapes, sizes and colours. They can be waxy, shiny, lobed, tooth-edged, spiky, etc. Veins can stem from one or more main veins and can be oriented in different directions.	What language are the children using? Are they describing colour, size and shape alone or are they observing leaf features such as stem and veins?
02	Resource sheet CLASSIFYING PLANTS AND ANIMALS 2	None of the plant parts mentioned are features of all plants – some plants have no roots (mosses), some have no flowers (ferns), some have no true leaves (cactus), and some have no stem (liverworts).	Do children think all plants have these parts? If not, can they give examples of plants without a certain feature?
03	Resource sheet CLASSIFYING PLANTS AND ANIMALS 3	Animals with backbones are called vertebrates. They are found on land, in ponds, oceans and other bodies of water, forests, mountains and even deserts. This group can be further divided into smaller groups by their characteristics, as: fish, amphibians, reptiles, birds, and mammals.	A good activity for a Teaching Assistant to observe how children sort the animals. What criteria are they using – do they think about key features such as fur, feathers, scales, etc?
04	Resource sheet CLASSIFYING PLANTS AND ANIMALS 4	Animals without backbones are called invertebrates and these make up about 97% of the animal kingdom. These animals are found in lands, ponds, oceans and other water bodies. They are six groups of invertebrates: annelids (segmented worms, leeches), molluscs (snails, limpets), arthropods (insects, crabs, centipedes and spiders), coelenterates (jellyfish, anemones), echinoderms (starfish, sea urchins) and protozoa (single cell organisms).	The activity is named 'minibeasts'; however, the proper name is invertebrates – are children using this word? Do children recognise differences in legs, shell, body segments?
05	Resource sheet CLASSIFYING PLANTS AND ANIMALS 5	Microorganisms are very tiny living things. They are so small that you need a microscope to see them. Microorganisms are all around us, in the air, in our bodies and in water. Some microorganisms are harmful to us, but others are helpful to us. There are three types of microorganism: viruses, bacteria, and some fungi.	Are children using any of the following vocabulary – 'microorganism', 'bacteria', 'virus' or 'fungi'? Where do they suggest we can find them?
06	Resource sheet CLASSIFYING PLANTS AND ANIMALS 6	A key is a set of questions about the characteristics of living things. By answering the questions, a key can be used to identify a living thing or to decide which group it belongs to. Questions are based on observable features and must be answered with either yes or no. Careful observations are needed to correctly identify things.	Do children make careful observations? Can they name the invertebrate as a harvestman?

LESSON ACTIVITY CARDS:

YEAR 6
CLASSIFYING PLANTS AND ANIMALS:
01 – LEAVES

why&how?

Examine the leaves.
What can you see?

Can you sort them into groups?
What heading would each group have?

Could you sort them a different way?
What heading would each group have?

YEAR 6
CLASSIFYING PLANTS AND ANIMALS:
02 – PARTS OF PLANTS

why&how?

Look at the cards.
Can you name each plant part?

Sort the cards into parts that all plants
have and parts that some plants have.

Describe the strangest plant you have heard of.
Why is it strange?

YEAR 6
CLASSIFYING PLANTS AND ANIMALS:
03 – VERTEBRATES

why&how?

Examine the cards.
Can you sort the animals into groups?

What heading would each group have?

Can you sort them a different way?
What heading would each group have?

YEAR 6
CLASSIFYING PLANTS AND ANIMALS:
04 – MINIBEASTS

why&how?

Observe the cards.
What is the name for this set of animals?

How are they the same?
How are they different?

Can you sort them into groups?
What heading would each group have?

YEAR 6
CLASSIFYING PLANTS AND ANIMALS:
05 – MICROORGANISMS

why&how?

Look closely at the pictures.
What do these pictures show?

Where would you find them?

How are they different and
how are they the same?

YEAR 6
CLASSIFYING PLANTS AND ANIMALS:
06 – IDENTIFICATION KEY

why&how?

Look at the picture.
Describe this insect.

Can you use the identification key to name it?

Explain why it isn't a spider.

Download a pdf of these activity cards from our website:
pstt.org.uk/eee-resources

CHALLENGING MISCONCEPTIONS:

1) All sea creatures are fish.

2) Spiders are insects.

3) All plants have flowers.

1) Fish are cold-blooded – they cannot regulate their own temperature, and they breathe through gills. Animals such as whales are warm-blooded and come to the surface to breathe air using lungs. Whales do have hair on their skin, which they usually lose at birth. They feed their young with milk.

• Children should compare a cod and a whale – what is the same, what is different?

• How do fish breathe? Dissect fish gills. (Use food quality fish. Use scissors and cover all surfaces in newspaper.)

How do whales breathe? Research.

2) All insects have six legs and three body parts.

• Observe spiders in the local habitat. Carefully catch one in a specimen pot or take photos in order to observe closely. Look carefully at the body segments and number of legs.

• Compare spiders with beetles or ants. What is the same? What is different?

3) Flowers create new plants. Non-flowering plants include ferns, mosses and conifers. These plants create new plants using spores.

• Observe the growth of ferns over time. Examine spores on the underside of fern leaves with a microscope. There are also good video clips of ferns releasing spores.

• Observe the growth of conifers over time. Examine cones and seeds produced. Compare the cones produced by conifers to fruits produced by flowering plants.

QUESTIONS CHILDREN MAY ASK:

1) Are micro-organisms germs?

2) What is the difference between reptiles and amphibians?

3) Are there any plants with no roots?

1) Microorganisms are very tiny living things. They are so small that you need a microscope to see them. Microorganisms are all around us: in the air, in our bodies and in water. There are three types of microorganism: viruses, bacteria and some types of fungi. Some microorganisms are harmful to us, but others are helpful to us. 'Germs' is the word we use to describe microorganisms that are harmful or cause disease.

• Children to match microorganism to its effect – cold, making bread rise, sore throat, healthy tummy, yoghurt making, cheese making, chicken pox, flu, conjunctivitis, athlete's foot, vaccinations, antibiotics, decay.

• In pairs, research one of the above in more detail.

2) Reptiles and amphibians are both vertebrates. Reptiles are cold-blooded animals. They typically lay hard-shelled eggs and have skin covered with scales or bony plates. Some examples of reptiles are: alligators, crocodiles, lizards, snakes, turtles, and tortoises. Amphibians are animals that can live on land or in water. They spend part of their lives under water breathing through gills and part of their lives on land breathing with lungs. Amphibians have skin and no scales. Most amphibians lay eggs in the water. Some examples of amphibians are: frogs, toads, salamanders and newts.

• Observe, sketch and label physical features of live examples of each class of animal. Compare.

• Produce a fact file on either an amphibian or a reptile including details of physical features, habitat and life cycle.

• Play 'Guess Who' – each child to have an animal name stuck to their backs. Each child has to ask yes/no questions based on physical features, reproduction, habitat, etc., in order to identify the animal stuck onto their back. Each child can ask each other member of the class one question only and sit down as soon as their animal is correctly identified.

• Play Crazy Creatures: Everyone has a piece of paper and folds it in four, with the folds running widthways across the paper. On the top panel draw an animal's head, making the two lines of the neck carry over into the second panel. Players fold the panel so it cannot be seen, and pass it to another child. The next player draws the top of the animal's body and passes the paper on. The third player draws the rest of the body, and the fourth draws the legs and feet.

The last player opens up the creature and decides where it might live and whether the creature is a mammal, reptile, fish, bird or insect based on the physical characteristics that can be seen. What does it eat and how? How does it reproduce? Once they've made their decisions, share with the rest of the class.

3) Moss and liverworts have no roots, instead they have thin root-like growths that help anchor the plant. Because they don't have roots or stems to transport water, mosses and liverworts dry out very quickly, so they are usually found in moist habitats.

• Examine moss using a digital microscope, focusing on root-like growths. Compare with roots of common plants.

• Search for moss in the local habitat – where is it found? Compare the growth to that of a common flower, e.g. daisy, depth of roots, structure of plant – parts, size, etc.

02 – PARTS OF PLANTS

Look at the cards.

Can you name each plant part?

Sort the cards into parts that all plants have and parts that some plants have.

Describe the strangest plant you have heard of. Why is it strange?

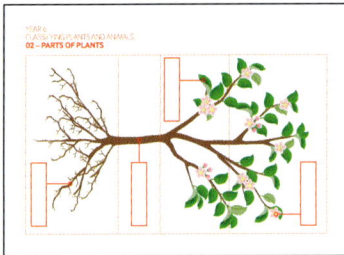

03 – VERTEBRATES

YEAR 6
CLASSIFYING PLANTS AND ANIMALS:
03 – VERTEBRATES

why&
how?

Examine the cards.

Can you sort the animals into groups?

What heading would each group have?

Can you sort them a different way?
What heading would each group have?

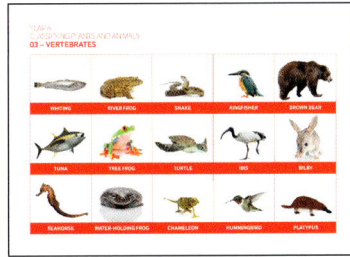

04 – MINIBEASTS

Observe the cards.

What is the name for this set of animals?

How are they the same?
How are they different?

Can you sort them into groups?
What heading would each group have?

05 – MICROORGANISMS

Look closely at the pictures.

What do these pictures show?

Where would you find them?

**How are they different and
how are they the same?**

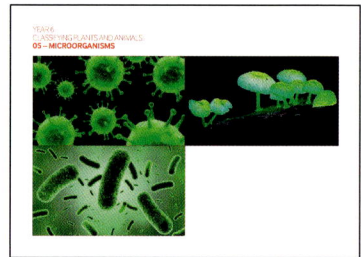

06 – IDENTIFICATION KEY

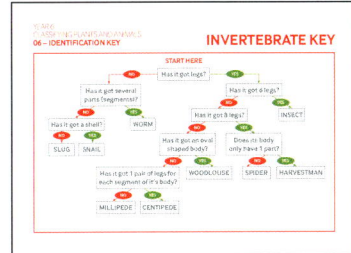

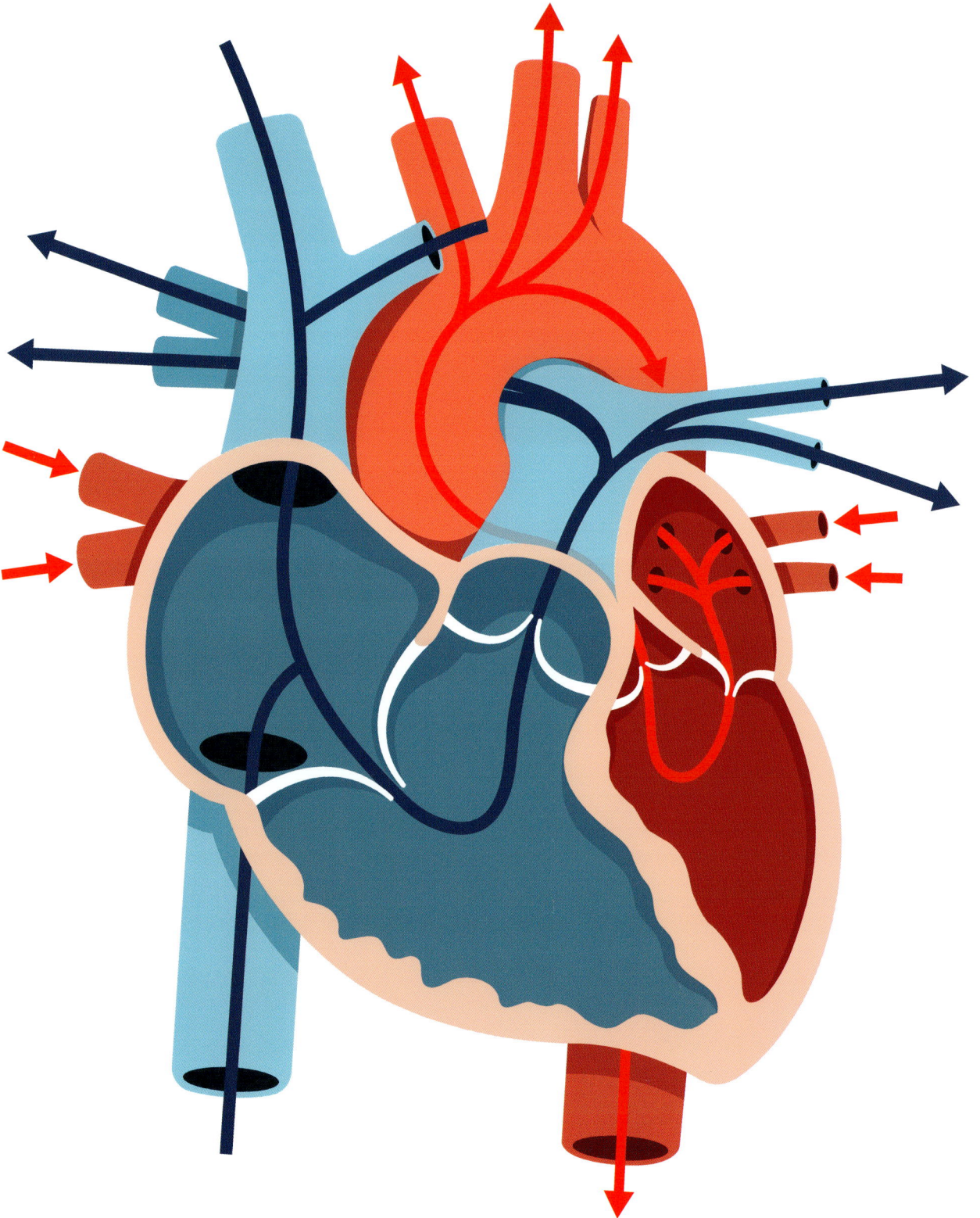

CIRCULATORY SYSTEM AND HEALTH

Key concepts

- Nutrients and water are transported via the circulatory system within animals, including humans.

- Diet, exercise, drugs and lifestyle have an impact on the way our bodies function.

Key vocabulary:

Circulatory system	Vein	Water
Heart	Pump	Diet
Blood	Oxygen	Exercise
Blood vessel	Carbon dioxide	Drugs
Artery	Lungs	Lifestyle
Capillary	Nutrients	

Activity	Resources required	Background knowledge	What to look out for
01	Plain paper.	A human heart is a muscular organ, roughly the size of the human's fist and located just to the left of the breastbone. It ensures that blood flows around our body. Poor diet, lack of exercise and drugs can all adversely affect the function of the heart.	Are children aware of what their heart looks like, how big it is and where it is located?
02	Model blood made from red jelly beans (enough to almost fill container), a white marshmallow, a teaspoon of uncooked rice, cooking oil to fill small, clear plastic bottle.	Blood transports materials around the body and protects against disease. It contains: • Red blood cells, which transport oxygen. • White blood cells, which protect against disease. • Blood platelets, which help the blood to clot and repair cuts. • Plasma, which is a liquid that carries these cells. It also transports dissolved nutrients.	Which human blood structures and their functions are children aware of?
03	Resource sheet CIRCULATORY SYSTEM AND HEALTH 3	The circulatory system is made up of the heart, blood vessels and blood. The heart keeps all the blood in the circulatory system flowing. Blood travels through a network of blood vessels to everywhere in the body. Arteries carry blood away from the heart and transport oxygen and useful nutrients to the body's cells (shown in red). After the oxygen has been used up, veins take blood back to the heart (shown in blue) where it is pumped to the lungs to excrete carbon dioxide and take in oxygen.	Can children name any of the blood vessels?
04	Resource sheet CIRCULATORY SYSTEM AND HEALTH 4	The food we eat, the exercise we do, the hours we sleep and the drugs we take all impact our health. A healthy diet, active life style, adequate sleep (9–11 hours per night for school-aged children) and prescribed drugs all contribute to a healthy body. Too much fat, sugar and salt, too little exercise, inadequate sleep and drug abuse all contribute to an unhealthy body.	Can children sort the pictures correctly? Do they recognise the effects on body and mind – concentration, mood, etc? Can they describe steps to take to improve health?
05	A range of foods – canned, fresh, dried. Some healthy, some not.	Foods containing a high proportion of fat, sugar or salt are considered unhealthy and these should be limited. Foods high in vitamins, minerals, fibre and protein are considered healthy and should be eaten regularly. See the 'Eatwell Plate' for guidance.	What misconceptions do the children hold about food?
06	None needed.	Drugs are any substances that have an effect on body functions. Drugs can be helpful, e.g. medicines for asthma, diabetes. Some drugs are illegal or controlled as they harm your body, e.g. tobacco, alcohol, cocaine. Even prescribed medicines and painkillers can be dangerous if taken incorrectly.	Children sometimes fail to recognise that medicines are drugs and that these can be dangerous if taken incorrectly.

LESSON ACTIVITY CARDS:

YEAR 6
CIRCULATORY SYSTEM AND HEALTH
01 – THE HEART

why & how?

Draw a picture.
**What does our heart look like?
How big is it?**

What does it do?

**Why might it not work properly?
Think of as many reasons as possible.**

YEAR 6
CIRCULATORY SYSTEM AND HEALTH
02 – BLOOD AND BLOOD VESSELS

why & how?

Observe the blood.
What can you see?

What does our blood do?

**Can you name any blood components
and describe what they do?**

YEAR 6
CIRCULATORY SYSTEM AND HEALTH
03 – CIRCULATORY SYSTEM

why & how?

Look carefully at the picture.
What does it show?

Can you name any parts?

**Can you explain what the
red and blue represent?**

YEAR 6
CIRCULATORY SYSTEM AND HEALTH
04 – HEALTH

why & how?

Look carefully at the pictures.
Can you sort them into healthy and unhealthy?

**What words can you use to describe the appearance
of an unhealthy person? What words can you use to
describe the appearance of a healthy person?**

How could an unhealthy person become healthy?

YEAR 6
CIRCULATORY SYSTEM AND HEALTH
05 – DIET

why & how?

Examine the foods.
Can you sort the food into groups?

What headings should be put on the groups?

**Can you sort the foods another way?
What would the headings be?
How many different ways can you sort these foods?**

YEAR 6
CIRCULATORY SYSTEM AND HEALTH
06 – DRUGS

why & how?

What are drugs?

Can you name four?

How do they affect your body?

Download a pdf of these activity cards from our website:
pstt.org.uk/eee-resources

CHALLENGING MISCONCEPTIONS:

1) The heart makes blood.

2) Blood travels in one loop between the heart and the body.

3) Fat is bad for our bodies.

1) The heart is mainly comprised of cardiac muscle. Most of our blood is made in the bone marrow inside our bones.

• Show children a real animal's heart – lamb heart does not offend religious groups. Dissect for children, or allow children to dissect in small groups (see 'Questions children may ask: Q1'). Show children the heart muscle, the four chambers of the heart and the vessels entering and leaving the heart.

2) Children can often view the heart to body route of blood as a single loop, and do not realise that circulation follows a double loop. Blood leaves the heart and goes into the lungs to take up oxygen and excrete carbon dioxide. It then travels back to the heart in order to be pumped around the rest of the body.

• Show children the different chambers of the heart, and how one side of the heart has thinner muscle (needs to pump to the lungs only) and one has much thicker muscle (needs to pump to the whole of the rest of the body). Use a mix of real hearts, animation/video and diagrams.

• Ask children to present a demonstration of how blood is circulated around the body as a drama or role play acting as red blood cells.

3) Children think all fat and sugar is bad for their health and do not appreciate that our bodies needs small amounts of these.

• Investigate the Eatwell Plate and the suggested proportions of the different food classes for each meal.

• Research recommended daily allowances (RDA) for different food classes and investigate the nutritional information and % RDA of favourite foods

• Research the function of each food group in our bodies. Why do we need some fat? Why do we need some sugar?

QUESTIONS CHILDREN MAY ASK:

1) How does the heart beat?

2) What would happen if we didn't have any blood?

3) How do you get fat?

1) The heart is a muscular pump, which is controlled by the medulla in the brain. Muscle on the left side contracts to pump oxygenated blood around the body. Muscle on the right side contracts to pump deoxygenated blood to the lungs. The Lub-DUB sound of a heartbeat is made by the valves in the heart closing to prevent backflow. The first sound is made by the closing of the valves between the atria (top chambers) and the ventricles (lower chambers) and the second louder sound is made by the closing of the valves at the bases of the pulmonary artery and aorta.

• Watch a video/animation of the action of the heart.

• Children could dissect a heart in groups of 4. Tables need to be covered in newspaper and scissors used for dissection, not knives. Lamb hearts should be used to avoid offending religious groups. A note should be sent to parents beforehand in case they would like their child to opt out (research using reference books can be completed instead). Children should observe and sketch the whole heart first, annotating their sketches with observations of what they can see, smell, feel and any questions they have at this point. Each group is allowed to make four cuts – one per group member. Each cut should be discussed beforehand – what do they expect to find? – and afterwards – what can they observe now? Share observations as a class, highlighting key points such as the thick muscle on the left hand side compared to the thinner muscle on the right. Wrap all waste in the newspaper and dispose of as food waste. Children to wash their hands thoroughly and teacher to disinfect scissors.

• In groups, model the action of the heart as a drama/role play.

2) Blood transports materials around the body and protects against disease. It contains red blood cells, which transport oxygen (and some of the waste carbon dioxide), white blood cells, which protect against disease, platelets, which help the blood to clot and repair cuts and plasma, which is a liquid that carries these cells and transports dissolved nutrients.

• Make a model of each component using modelling clay or dough. Research the function of components and present to class as a mockumentary.

• Make models of blood using red jelly beans/ Smarties/Skittles as red blood cells (5 million per microliter), white marshmallows as white blood cells (should be larger than the red blood cells with a ratio of 1:700 white cells to red cells), uncooked rice as platelets (1:15 platelets to red cells), and cooking oil as the plasma. Discuss the function of each part as you make the models.

3) Fat is stored when the body takes in more calories than it uses. Foods high in sugar and fat have more calories. An active lifestyle burns calories.

• Research the calories contained in the children's favourite meals and compare with the recommended daily allowance, and with calories burned off through various activities such as cycling and running.

• Plan a healthy, balanced meal. Extend this activity by planning a meal for someone requiring a particular diet such as a person with diabetes or an Olympic athlete.

03 – CIRCULATORY SYSTEM

YEAR 6
CIRCULATORY SYSTEM AND HEALTH:
03 – CIRCULATORY SYSTEM

why&
how?

Look carefully at the picture.

What does it show?

Can you name any parts?

**Can you explain what the
red and blue represent?**

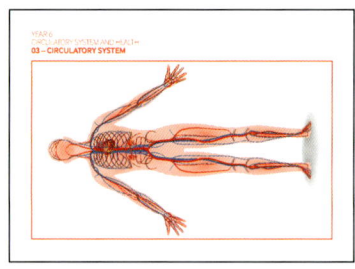

04 – HEALTH

YEAR 6
CIRCULATORY SYSTEM AND HEALTH:
04 – HEALTH

why&
how?

Look carefully at the pictures.

Can you sort them into healthy and unhealthy?

What words can you use to describe the appearance of an unhealthy person? What words can you use to describe the appearance of a healthy person?

How could an unhealthy person become healthy?

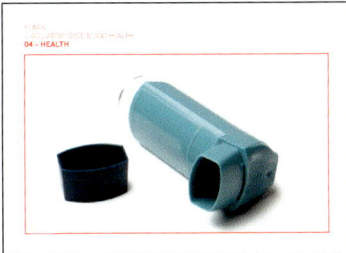

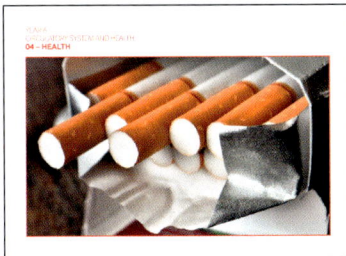

Mammal

Bird

Arthropod

Reptile

Bony fish

Annelid   Echinoderm   Amphibian

Cartilaginous fishes

Molluscs

Nematode

Agnatha

Coelenterata

Flatworm

Protist

Sponge

Protist

EVOLUTION AND INHERITANCE

Key concepts

- Living things have changed over time.

- Fossils provide information about living things that inhabited the Earth millions of years ago.

- Living things produce offspring of the same kind, but normally offspring vary and are not identical to their parents.

- Characteristics of offspring can be inherited or non-inherited.

- Adaptation may lead to evolution.

- Animals and plants are adapted to suit their environment in different ways.

- Physical and behavioural characteristics of plants and animals are related to their survival or extinction.

Key vocabulary:

Evolution	Adapted	Vary
Suited	Adaptation	Variation
Fossils	Offspring	Inherit
Environment	Characteristic	Inheritance

Activity	Resources required	Background knowledge	What to look out for
01	Samples of fossils.	The only reason we know about dinosaurs and other extinct animals is because their remains have been preserved as fossils. Usually the bodies of dead animals and other living things are destroyed completely by decay, but sometimes they become buried in a way that stops decay. Over time, these may become fossils.	Children should know the process of fossil formation from year 3; this will need repeating if not. Do children know why fossils are useful to us and the evidence they provide?
02	Resource sheet EVOLUTION AND INHERITANCE 2	Inherited features are those that are passed down from our parents and include eye colour, hair colour, height, skin colour. Some features are not passed on from our parents and are influenced by our environment, e.g. favourite food, hobbies and weight.	Are children aware that offspring inherit features from both their mum and dad?
03	Resource sheet EVOLUTION AND INHERITANCE 3	Every plant or animal lives in a habitat. A habitat is another name for their local environment. The animals and plants in one habitat are suited to live there and may not be able to survive in other places. A woodland owl would not survive in a desert habitat because there is little water available, there would be nowhere for it to shelter and the temperatures would be much warmer than it would be used to.	Do children realise a habitat provides the right shelter, food and protection for an animal to live and reproduce comfortably?
04	A cactus and a different plant. Hand lenses. Real plants should be used rather than pictures.	The only thing all plants have in common is that they all produce their own food using energy from the Sun. Plants are extremely varied – some have leaves, some do not, some have flowers, some do not, some have roots, some do not, some have a stem, some do not. All plants are adapted to survive the conditions that their habitat provides such as light, water, temperature and animals.	Watch the vocabulary that children are using – how do they describe the spines and stem of the cactus? Do they realise that spines help to conserve water and protect against animals?
05	Resource sheet EVOLUTION AND INHERITANCE 5	Animals are adapted to their habitats. An adaptation is a modification or change in the animal's body or behaviour that helps it to survive. An African elephant, for example, lives in a hot habitat and has very large ears that it flaps to keep cool. A polar bear, on the other hand, lives in a cold habitat and has thick fur to keep warm. Hedgehogs hibernate over the winter to survive harsh conditions and lack of food.	Do children realise that a penguin's shape is streamlined for faster swimming and diving in order to catch their food? Or do they recognise that they have a thick layer of blubber to keep them warm in icy water?
06	Resource sheet EVOLUTION AND INHERITANCE 6	Camouflage is how some animals protect themselves from predators. Camouflage makes them less easy to see and more likely to survive and reproduce.	Are children using the word 'camouflage'? Do they realise that the dark moth is more likely to survive and reproduce?

LESSON ACTIVITY CARDS:

YEAR 6
EVOLUTION AND INHERITANCE
01 – FOSSILS

why & how?

Examine the samples.

What can you see?

How were these created?

Why are they useful to us?

YEAR 6
EVOLUTION AND INHERITANCE
02 – OFFSPRING

why & how?

Look at the pictures of mother and father.

How are they the same? How are they different?

Which child would they be most likely to produce? Why?

How might the child be different from their parents?

YEAR 6
EVOLUTION AND INHERITANCE
03 – HABITATS

why & how?

Examine the cards.

Can you match each animal and habitat?

Could it live somewhere else?

Why is the animal suited to this environment?

YEAR 6
EVOLUTION AND INHERITANCE
04 – PLANT ADAPTATIONS

why & how?

Observe the plants.

Can you name the plants?

How are they the same? How are they different?

Why does a cactus have spines?

YEAR 6
EVOLUTION AND INHERITANCE
05 – ANIMAL ADAPTATIONS

why & how?

Look closely at the pictures.

Can you describe the animals?

How are they different and how are they the same?

Why is a penguin shaped like that?

YEAR 6
EVOLUTION AND INHERITANCE
06 – PEPPERED MOTHS

why & how?

Look at the picture.

How many moths do you see?

Why is one moth harder to see?

What might happen to the light moth? What might happen to the dark moth?

Download a pdf of these activity cards from our website:
pstt.org.uk/eee-resources

CHALLENGING MISCONCEPTIONS:

1) Camels' humps store water.

2) Adaptations give animals what they need.

3) We evolved from monkeys.

1) Camels' humps store fat, not water.

- Children should research the adaptations of camels and other animals. See 'Questions number 1' on the opposite page for suggestions for this.

2) Adaptations occur all the time due to changes in our DNA – the building blocks of life. Many changes are 'invisible' and not seen in our appearance but can affect our abilities to survive. For example, people with BRCA gene variation have a higher likelihood of developing breast cancer. Some changes allow individuals to survive a challenge better than others and those individuals will have more offspring in the next generation. For example, a slightly darker colouring helped some peppered moths camouflage themselves better during the polluted industrial revolution, so they lived to reproduce and the number of darker coloured moths increased. Lighter ones were more easily spotted by predators, so not as many survived to reproduce.

- Either in the school hall or school grounds, children to choose a surface and design a moth to be camouflaged against that surface, then play a 'spot the moth' competition. Measure distance away from which moth eventually spotted. Which moths are more likely to survive and reproduce? Which moths are likely to be eaten and fail to reproduce?

3) Humans are more closely related to apes than monkeys. Monkeys, apes and humans all evolved from a common ancestor. Humans are not more evolved or special – each species of primate followed a different evolutionary path due to environment and needs.

- Show sketch of what the first primate looked like. What are the key changes from this to human and how did the change help us?

- Use the primate evolutionary/family tree to demonstrate how we are related to but not evolved from apes. Children can also look at the evolutionary tree for reptiles.

- Compare humans and apes. What is the same? What is different? Think about diet, appearance and behaviour. How are apes suited to their habitat? Would we survive in their habitat?

QUESTIONS CHILDREN MAY ASK:

1) Why do hedgehogs have spikes?

2) Which living things haven't evolved?

3) Is there such a thing as a man-made animal?'

1) Children will have lots of questions about the different features of animals and plants – both physical features and behaviour, e.g. why can't penguins fly? Why are some animals nocturnal? Why do cows have four stomachs?

- Allow children to follow their interests and research the adaptations of an animal or plant and its habitat. This work could be presented in many different ways – a non-chronological report in English, a 'habitat in a box' with accompanying notes, a computing multimedia presentation, labelled diagrams, etc.

- Follow up this research by giving children an extreme habitat, e.g. the Moon or a volcano, and ask them to create an animal or plant with adaptations to survive in that environment.

2) All species of plants and animals change over time due to genes mutating and being reshuffled in reproduction. However, this does not always mean big changes and some plants and animals have stayed roughly the same for millions of years as they are well suited to their environment.

- Investigate animals and plants such as coelacanths, nautilus, ginkgo biloba, crocodiles, platypus, horseshoe crabs and cycads. Where do they live? What are the conditions? Why have these species stayed roughly the same?

- Compare the habitats and features of the animals and plants above to animals and plants in danger of becoming extinct – Giant Panda, Vaquita porpoise, leatherback turtle, Magellanic penguin, polar bear and crested cow-wheat. Why are these species struggling? What adaptations would they need to survive?

3) Humans have used selective breeding to create animals and plants that have useful features and characteristics. Farmers have used selective breeding for centuries to increase milk yield in cattle, produce larger eggs from chickens and obtain more grain from wheat. Many different dog species have all been selectively bred from a common ancestor.

- Introduce the idea of inheritance using cross breed dogs – look at the offspring of a Labrador and a poodle and other examples.

- Use Little Miss and Mr Men – characteristics are passed onto offspring by both parents. Draw what the offspring of Mr Strong and Little Miss Dotty might look like.

- Investigate how species of plants or animals have been changed by selective breeding – either for usefulness or appearance. For example, how does an ancient pig compare to the modern farm animal? Why has it been bred like this? How would the farmer produce even more muscle in future pigs? Compare modern sweetcorn to ancient corn. Why has it changed? How has it been changed? How would the gardener produce even sweeter kernels?

02 – OFFSPRING

YEAR 6
EVOLUTION AND INHERITANCE:
02 – OFFSPRING

why&
how?

Look at the pictures of mother and father.

How are they the same? How are they different?

**Which child would they be most
likely to produce? Why?**

**How might the child be different
from their parents?**

03 – HABITATS

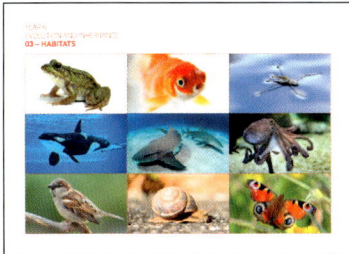

05 – ANIMAL ADAPTATIONS

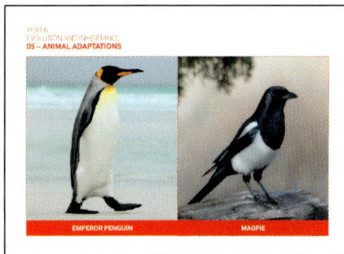

06 – PEPPERED MOTHS

ELECTRICITY – CHANGING CIRCUITS

Key concepts

- Energy is transferred from the power supply to the components of a circuit.

- The brightness of a lamp or the volume of a buzzer is associated with the number and voltage of cells used in the circuit.

- Recognised symbols are used to represent a simple circuit in a diagram.

Key vocabulary:

Electricity	Cell	Wire	Motor
Appliance	Battery	Crocodile clip	Conductor
Device	Positive	Bulb	Insulator
Electrical circuit	Negative	Bright	Metal
Complete circuit	Terminal	Dim	Non metal
Circuit diagram	Connect	Switch	Voltage
Circuit symbol	Connection	Buzzer	Current
Component	Short circuit	Volume	Resistance

Activity	Resources required	Background knowledge	What to look out for
01	Simple circuit with bulb.	A simple circuit is made of a cell, a bulb in a holder, and wires connected by crocodile clips. If the cell is missing, there would be no 'push' to make the current move around the circuit. If the bulb was missing, electric current would still flow around but none of the energy would be converted to light and it would cause a short circuit.	Can children correctly name components and explain the function of each? Children may think electricity comes from/is stored in the battery.
02	Simple circuit with buzzer.	A circuit may be changed by reducing/increasing or replacing components. More or fewer cells will mean the buzzer will be louder or quieter. More wires may slightly decrease the volume of the buzzer as each wire creates resistance. The buzzer may be changed for a motor or bulb and electrical energy be converted to movement or light instead of sound. A switch may be added to break/make a complete circuit.	Are children aware that buzzers, bulbs and motors can be louder, brighter and faster or quieter, dimmer and slower, according to the current of the circuit? What vocabulary are they using?
03	Simple circuit with bulb.	The bulb could be made brighter by adding more cells, or by using a cell with greater voltage. The brightness of a bulb can be measured by placing pieces of paper over the bulb until the light is no longer visible, or by covering the bulb with a cardboard tube and measuring the light inside using a light sensor.	Can children suggest ways to make the bulb brighter? Can they think of a practical way to measure brightness that doesn't rely on children's subjective opinions?
04	A range of cells of different shape, size and voltage.	Cells can be compared according to shape, size and voltage. Most have visible positive and negative terminals. Common chemical compositions inside the cell are lithium, zinc-carbon, zinc-chloride or alkaline, which use zinc and manganese oxide to generate power.	Are children using the word 'volt' or just comparing the cells on appearance alone?
05	Resource sheet CHANGING CIRCUITS 5, circuit components, simple circuit with buzzer.	There are standard symbols used when drawing circuit diagrams. See Resource sheet ELECTRICITY 5 – SYMBOLS. All components are joined by straight lines.	Can children correctly match the symbols to the components? Can they draw the circuit using the correct symbols and straight lines?
06	Resource sheet CHANGING CIRCUITS 6	Mains electricity can kill – never stick anything into sockets and children should ask an adult to plug in appliances. Faults in wiring can cause fires – wires should not trail across the floor where they might be damaged. Sockets should not be overloaded. Water is an excellent conductor of electricity and should be kept away from electrical appliances. Cells contain corrosive chemicals. If enough are connected in a circuit, they could cause an electric shock. Cells can become hot if short-circuited repeatedly.	Do children recognise key dangers of mains electricity? Are they aware that even 1.5 volt cells can be hazardous?

LESSON ACTIVITY CARDS:

YEAR 6
ELECTRICITY – CHANGING CIRCUITS
01 – CIRCUIT COMPONENTS

Look at the circuit.

What components can you name?

What is the function of each component?

What would happen if the cell was missing?
What would happen if the bulb was missing?

YEAR 6
ELECTRICITY – CHANGING CIRCUITS
02 – CHANGING CIRCUITS

Look at the circuit.

How could you change the circuit?

What effect would this have?

Can you think of another way to change the circuit?
What effect would this have?

YEAR 6
ELECTRICITY – CHANGING CIRCUITS
03 – BRIGHTER BULB

Look at the circuit.

How could you make the bulb brighter?

Can you think of more than one way?

How could you measure the brightness of a bulb?

YEAR 6
ELECTRICITY – CHANGING CIRCUITS
04 – CELLS

Look carefully at the cells.

What is the same about these cells?

What is different?

How would this affect the circuit?

YEAR 6
ELECTRICITY – CHANGING CIRCUITS
05 – SYMBOLS

Look carefully at the symbols and components.

Can you match each symbol to the correct circuit component?

Use the symbols to draw the circuit on the table.

How should these be joined?

YEAR 6
ELECTRICITY – CHANGING CIRCUITS
06 – SAFETY

Can you write three rules for using mains electricity safely?

Which parts of this circuit could be dangerous?

Why?

Download a pdf of these activity cards from our website:
pstt.org.uk/eee-resources

CHALLENGING MISCONCEPTIONS:

1) Electricity is stored in a battery.

2) I can make the bulb brighter by making the circuit bigger.

3) I can make the bulb brighter by using a bigger battery.

1) Energy is stored in a cell (a battery is made from more than one cell connected together). Charges (or electrons) already exist in the wires and are simply set in motion by the battery, in all parts of the circuit at the same time.

- Use the analogy of a pump pushing water around central heating or pond and show a working model. Pump and water is a very good analogy to use for explaining that the charge is present in all conducting materials (water is already all round the system), the function of wires (tubes for water to travel through), resistance (wider and narrower tubes), current (flow of water) and cell (water pump – the bigger the pump, the faster the flow). However, this analogy does not demonstrate the transfer of energy to bulbs and other components.

- Another analogy is the rope loop. A circuit is modelled as a big loop of rope held by a circle of children (conductive materials). One person is the battery and pushes the loop forwards while pulling the loop through their hands. The rope moving is the current. One child could be a bulb and resist the current by squeezing it – they will feel the transfer of energy to heat. In this analogy it's clear that energy is transferred very quickly, even though the rope can be moving quite slowly. This emphasises the idea that the charges are already there and they all start moving everywhere at the same time.

2) The bulb can be made brighter by adding more cells or using a cell with a higher voltage. In both these circumstances, the electrical energy is increased and this increases the push and makes the current flow faster. The bulb may get dimmer if the size of the circuit is increased by adding more wire or bulbs, as wires and bulbs cause resistance, which means that energy is transferred to heat and/or light.

- Allow children to investigate what happens as elements of a circuit are changed, as a fair test. Begin with the general question 'What affects the brightness of a bulb?' and brainstorm possibilities. Using post-It note planning, groups could each investigate a different variable, e.g. number of cells, length of wire, etc. Brightness of bulbs can be measured by placing pieces of paper over the bulb until the light is no longer visible, or by covering the bulb with a cardboard tube and measuring the light inside the tube using a light sensor.

3) Children think that the size of a bulb is proportional to the electrical energy stored inside. However, it is the voltage of a cell that determines this. A 6 V cell will give a bigger push than a 1.5 V cell.

- Compare the effect of different cells on a bulb. AA and AAA cells should produce the same current and light in a simple circuit.

- Compare the effect of multiple cells – added voltage will increase the brightness of the light. Warning: Using cell voltage that is higher than the bulb's rated voltage will cause the bulb to burn out or in some cases explode as the temperature will get too high.

QUESTIONS CHILDREN MAY ASK:

1) How does a battery make a bulb light up?

2) What is inside a battery?

3) How much electricity do you need for it to be dangerous?

1) There are particles called electrons in every part of a circuit and the cell causes these electrons to move around the circuit as a current. The filament of a bulb is made of very thin tungsten wire, which causes lots of resistance to the flow of electrons. Resistance is how easily the current flows around a circuit. The thin wire inhibits the flow of the electrons – there is friction between them and the atoms of the metal, which causes the wire to heat up and emit light.

• Use the analogy of traffic and roads to explain resistance. Using model cars and a drawing of a road, set up a bottleneck scenario, which represents the filament making the flow of current more difficult.

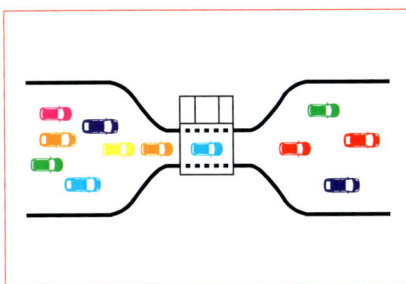

2) Most batteries contain two important parts: electrodes and an electrolyte. There are two electrodes in every battery, both made of conductive materials. One electrode, known as the cathode, connects to the positive end of the battery and the other electrode, known as the anode, connects to the negative end of the battery. The electrolyte is a liquid or gel-like substance that contains electrically charged particles and is in contact with both electrodes.

• Make a potato or lemon battery. A galvanised nail (zinc-coated) acts as the anode and a copper penny (pre-1992 pennies are higher in copper) or copper wire acts as the cathode, with the lemon juice/ potato juice acting as the electrolyte. Many lemons/potatoes will be needed to create enough current to light a bulb – measure the voltage as each lemon/potato is added.

3) Electrical current is the flow of charge through a circuit and is measured in amps. Currents over 10 milliamps (0.01 amp) are capable of producing a painful to severe shock, and currents over 100 milliamps are lethal. All mains electricity can kill.

• Use an ammeter to measure the current in simple circuits, comparing the current produced by different cells.

• Invite in an electrician to speak to children about the job and the hazards.

• Research the size of the currents in mains electricity and lightning.

05 – SYMBOLS

Look carefully at the symbols and components.

Can you match each symbol to the correct circuit component?

Use the symbols to draw the circuit on the table.

How should these be joined?

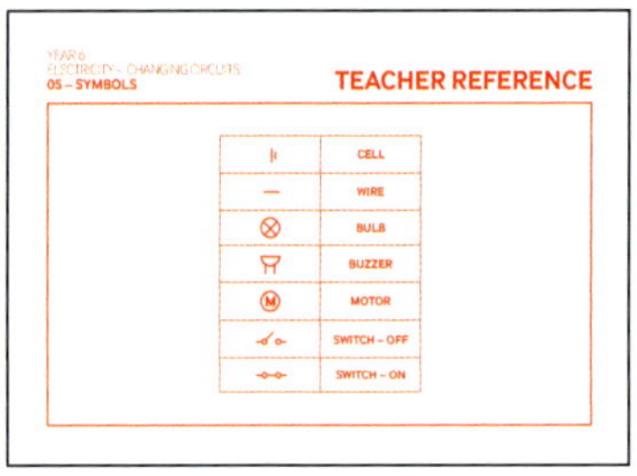

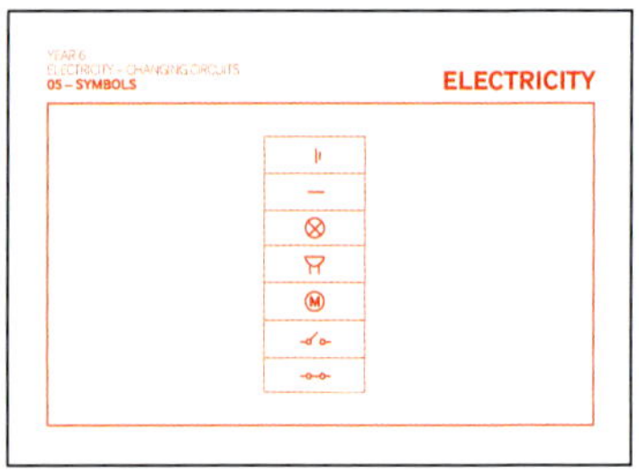

TEACHER REFERENCE

⊩	CELL
—	WIRE
⊗	BULB
⊻	BUZZER
Ⓜ	MOTOR
⌐⊶	SWITCH – OFF
-o-o-	SWITCH – ON

ELECTRICITY

⊩	
—	
⊗	
⊻	
Ⓜ	
⌐⊶	
-o-o-	

06 – SAFETY

why & how?

Can you write three rules for using
mains electricity safely?

Which parts of this circuit
could be dangerous?

Why?

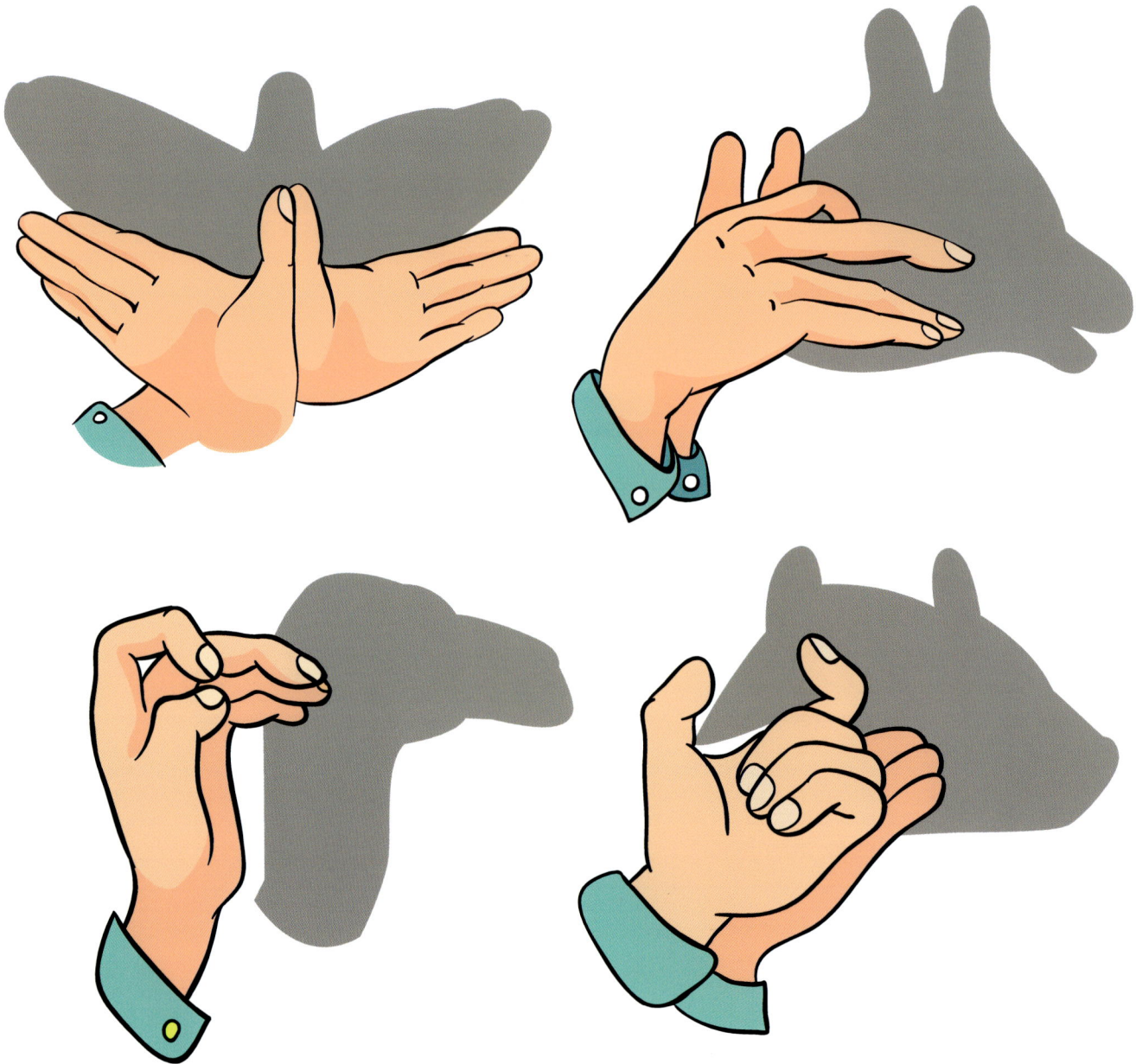

PROPERTIES OF LIGHT

Key concepts

- Light travels in straight lines.

- We see things because light travels from light sources to our eyes or from light sources to objects and then to our eyes.

- Shadows have the same shape as the objects that cast them.

Key vocabulary:

Light	Reflective	Direct
Light source	Mirror	Direction
Dark	Shadow	Transparent
Darkness	Block	Opaque
Reflect	Absorb	Translucent

Activity	Resources required	Background knowledge	What to look out for
01	Resource sheet PROPERTIES OF LIGHT 1 and thread.	Light travels in straight lines and can be reflected by different materials. We see objects because they give out or reflect light into our eyes. Dark is the absence of light. We cannot see if there is no light.	Children can think of sight as an active process of our eyes. Do children recognise that we need light in order to see, not just our eyes? Can they use the term 'dark' correctly?
02	Periscope.	Light travels in straight lines and can be reflected by different materials. Mirrors are very good reflectors of light. The image we see in the periscope is created by light being reflected by objects into the top of the periscope and then being reflected by a sequence of mirrors inside the periscope to our eyes.	Do children use the word 'reflect'? Do they describe the light as traveling down the periscope or think our 'sight' travels up?
03	A torch and range of materials – some very reflective, some not.	All materials we can see reflect light or we would not be able to see them. Some materials are better at reflecting light – pale and bright colours reflect light better whereas dark colours tend to absorb more rays. Very smooth surfaces reflect light in a more regular way and appear shiny.	Children may think that all non-shiny materials do not reflect light.
04	Resource sheet PROPERTIES OF LIGHT 4	Shadows are created when objects block light. The shadow will be the same shape as the object as light travels in straight lines. However, the shadow may be a different size and colour depending on the angle and distance of the light source and the original colour of the object.	Children may think that objects 'give out dark'. Do children link shadows to a light source and use the word 'block'?
05	Cardboard 'S', torch, surface for shadow to fall on. This activity should be set up in the darkest area of the classroom.	Shadows are always the same shape as the object blocking the light and all opaque objects produce a black shadow. This is because shadows are created by the object blocking light, which travels in straight lines. The size of the shadow can be changed by changing the distance or angle of the light source.	Do children link the shape of the shadow with the fact that light travels in straight lines?
06	Resource sheet PROPERTIES OF LIGHT 6	Shadows are always on the opposite side of an object to the light source. They will be the same shape as the object and will be black if the object is opaque. This is because they are created by the object blocking light, which travels in straight lines.	Are children drawing a shadow on the opposite side of the object? Is it linked to the object? Is it black? Can they explain why the shadow will appear like this?

LESSON ACTIVITY CARDS:

YEAR 6
PROPERTIES OF LIGHT:
01 – SIGHT

why &
how?

Can we see in the dark?

Why/why not?

Use the thread to show how light travels
and lets the child see the book.

YEAR 6
PROPERTIES OF LIGHT:
02 – PERISCOPE

why &
how?

Look through the periscope.
What can you see?

How is it different from what you
see without the periscope?

How does the periscope change what you see?

YEAR 6
PROPERTIES OF LIGHT:
03 – REFLECTED LIGHT

why &
how?

Shine a torch on each material.
Describe what happens to the light each time.

Can you sort them into those that are not
reflective, a little reflective and very reflective?

Why are they different?

YEAR 6
PROPERTIES OF LIGHT:
04 – SHADOWS

why &
how?

Look carefully at the cards.
Can you match the correct shadows to the objects?

What is the same about the shadow and the object?
What is different?

What is a shadow?

YEAR 6
PROPERTIES OF LIGHT:
05 – SHADOW OF SHAPE

why &
how?

Make a shadow using the cardboard shape and a torch.
What shape and colour is the shadow?

Can you make the shadow a different size? How?

Can you make the shadow a different shape?
Why/why not?

YEAR 6
PROPERTIES OF LIGHT:
06 – ADDING SHADOWS

why &
how?

Add a shadow to the picture.
Where would the shadow be?

What shape and colour would it be?

Why?

Download a pdf of these activity cards from our website:
pstt.org.uk/eee-resources

CHALLENGING MISCONCEPTIONS:

1) Without light it is hard to see.

2) Light shines from our eyes.

3) Shadows are formed when objects give off dark.

1+2) Without light it is impossible to see. We see objects because they emit light or they reflect light into our eyes.

• Use cardboard tubes to cut off light. Try reading a book down a cardboard tube pressed against the page. Cut a notch out of the book end of the tube. Now try reading – some light will mean some vision. Enlarge the notch to let in more light and try reading – more light means better vision.

3) Shadows are formed when an object blocks light.

• Ask children to find objects that are transparent, translucent and opaque and compare what happens to the light when a torch is shone through them onto a screen/whiteboard..

QUESTIONS CHILDREN MAY ASK:

1) Why can't shadows be different colours?

2) Why does the shadow get bigger when you move the torch?

3) How do we see things?

1) White light is comprised of all the colours of the rainbow. We see colour because objects reflect light of that colour into our eyes and absorb the rest. Coloured translucent objects reflect some of the colour light and allow some light to transmit through to the other side to form a coloured shadow, the rest of the light is absorbed. Opaque objects block all light, allowing none through.

• Compare the shadows formed by opaque and translucent objects, include coloured translucent objects.

• Create coloured shadows using opaque objects by using a blue light, a green light and a red light, all shining onto a white board. Lights need to be in this order, play around with the positions until the whitest light possible is made on the whiteboard. Hold a pencil close to the whiteboard, adjusting the distance until you can see three coloured shadows. A cyan shadow is formed by the pencil blocking the red light (cyan light = blue light and green light). A magenta shadow is formed by pencil blocking the green light (magenta light = red light and blue light). And a yellow shadow is formed by the pencil blocking the blue light (yellow light = green light and red light).

2) Shadows grow bigger and fuzzier as the object moves closer to the light source, and smaller and sharper as the object moves farther away. This is because the nearer the light source an object is, the more light it blocks.

• Demonstrate this using diagrams, drawing straight lines from light source to object and beyond to illustrate how the amount of light blocked changes as the object is moved nearer or further away. Or use the BBC Science Clips animation www.bbc.co.uk/schools/scienceclips/ages/7_8/light_shadows.shtml

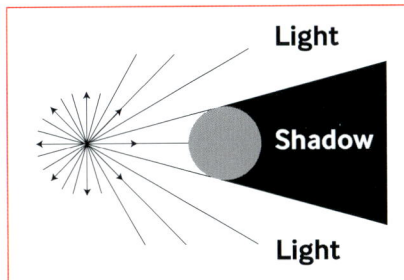

• Investigate the question 'What affects the size of a shadow' using the post-it notes to identify all the possible variables. Each group could investigate a different variable — distance of object to light source, distance of object to screen, brightness of light source, size of object, etc.

3) We see objects when they emit light or reflect light into our eyes.

• Use the cardboard tube from Challenging Misconceptions 1 and 2 on previous page to demonstrate how light bounces from objects into our eyes.

01 – SIGHT

YEAR 6
PROPERTIES OF LIGHT:
01 – SIGHT

why & how?

Can we see in the dark?

Why/why not?

Use the thread to show how light travels and lets the child see the book.

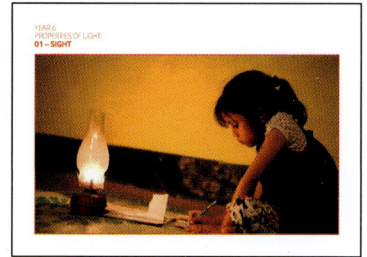

04 – SHADOWS

YEAR 6
PROPERTIES OF LIGHT:
04 – SHADOWS

why & how?

Look carefully at the cards.
Can you match the correct shadows to the objects?

**What is the same about the shadow and the object?
What is different?**

What is a shadow?

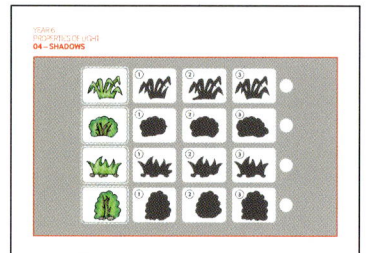